PAKISTAN NATIONAL URBAN ASSESSMENT
PIVOTING TOWARD SUSTAINABLE URBANIZATION

AUGUST 2024

ASIAN DEVELOPMENT BANK

 Creative Commons Attribution 3.0 IGO license (CC BY 3.0 IGO)

© 2024 Asian Development Bank
6 ADB Avenue, Mandaluyong City, 1550 Metro Manila, Philippines
Tel +63 2 8632 4444; Fax +63 2 8636 2444
www.adb.org

Some rights reserved. Published in 2024.

ISBN 978-92-9270-824-5 (print); 978-92-9270-825-2 (PDF); 978-92-9270-826-9 (e-book)
Publication Stock No. TCS240377-2
DOI: http://dx.doi.org/10.22617/TCS240377-2

The views expressed in this publication are those of the authors and do not necessarily reflect the views and policies of the Asian Development Bank (ADB) or its Board of Governors or the governments they represent.

ADB does not guarantee the accuracy of the data included in this publication and accepts no responsibility for any consequence of their use. The mention of specific companies or products of manufacturers does not imply that they are endorsed or recommended by ADB in preference to others of a similar nature that are not mentioned.

By making any designation of or reference to a particular territory or geographic area in this document, ADB does not intend to make any judgments as to the legal or other status of any territory or area.

This publication is available under the Creative Commons Attribution 3.0 IGO license (CC BY 3.0 IGO) https://creativecommons.org/licenses/by/3.0/igo/. By using the content of this publication, you agree to be bound by the terms of this license. For attribution, translations, adaptations, and permissions, please read the provisions and terms of use at https://www.adb.org/terms-use#openaccess.

This CC license does not apply to non-ADB copyright materials in this publication. If the material is attributed to another source, please contact the copyright owner or publisher of that source for permission to reproduce it. ADB cannot be held liable for any claims that arise as a result of your use of the material.

Please contact pubsmarketing@adb.org if you have questions or comments with respect to content, or if you wish to obtain copyright permission for your intended use that does not fall within these terms, or for permission to use the ADB logo.

Corrigenda to ADB publications may be found at http://www.adb.org/publications/corrigenda.

Notes:
In this publication, "$" refers to United States dollars.
The fiscal year of the Government of Pakistan ends on 30 June. "FY" before a calendar year denotes the year in which the fiscal year ends, e.g., FY2023 ends on 30 June 2023.

Cover design by Claudette Rodrigo.

 Printed on recycled paper

Contents

Tables, Figures, and Boxes	v
Acknowledgments	vii
Abbreviations	ix
Executive Summary	x
Urban Sector Overview	**1**
Demographics and Urbanization	1
Economic Environment	15
Social Equity Profile	23
Urban Governance	27
Urban Planning	37
Municipal Finances	40
Safety and Security	42
Cultural Heritage and Tourism	42
Climate Assessment	**44**
Background	44
Climate Change and Disaster Risks	44
Climate Change Policy, Legal, and Institutional Framework	45
Climate Change and the Urban Sector	46
Climate Resilience Through Adaptation and Mitigation	47
Urban Needs Assessment	**49**
Housing	49
Water and Sanitation	51
Energy Supply and Demand	56
Solid Waste Management	58
Urban Transport	61
Pollution	64

Urban Development Analysis — 65
    Land Use Management — 65
    Megacities—Karachi and Lahore — 67
    Other Major Cities — 69
    Good Practices — 70
    ADB in Pakistan — 71

Urban Development Futures — 73
    Urban Governance — 73
    Sustainable Urban Planning — 75
    Role of Development Partners — 77
    Urban Development Scenarios — 78

Appendix — 80
    Pakistan's Budget Allocation Systems — 80

Tables, Figures, and Boxes

Tables

1	Share of Each Province's Largest City in National, Provincial, and Urban Populations, 2017	5
2	Share of Urban Localities by Population Size in National Urban Population, 2017 Census	9
3	Annual Population Change of Major Cities, 1972–2017	9
4	Migration Profile of Provinces and Major Cities or Districts, 2020	10
5	Merchandise Exports and Imports, FY2017–FY2022	19
6	Major Exports and Imports, FY2021 and FY2022	20
7	Provincial Economic Output, FY2014–FY2020	21
8	Urban Population in Major Cities with Access to Water and Sanitation, 2020	52
9	Wastewater Treatment Plants in Karachi's Industrial Sector, 2019	56

Figures

1	National and Provincial Populations, 1998–2023	2
2	Average Annual Population Growth, 1981–2023	3
3	Population Density, 1998–2023	4
4	National Population Age and Sex Composition, 1998–2020	6
5	Urban and Rural Population Shares of Total Population, 1998–2023	7
6	Total, Urban, and Rural Population Growth Rates, 1998–2023	7
7	National and Per-Province Urban Population, 1998–2023	8
8	Urban Centers Distribution, 2017	12
9	Urban Footprint, 2016	13
10	Urban Encroachments into Agricultural Lands, 2017	13
11	Emerging Linear Urban Developments in Punjab and Khyber Pakhtunkhwa, 2017	14
12	Growth in Gross Domestic Product, FY2001–FY2023	15
13	Annual Sector Growth, FY2017–FY2023	17
14	Sector Shares in Gross Domestic Product, FY2017–FY2022	17
15	Changes in Sector Shares in Gross Domestic Product, 1950–2021	18
16	Changes in Sector Shares in Employment, 1963–2021	18
17	Employment per Sector and Province, FY2021	22
18	Employment per Sector in Major Cities, FY2021	23
19	National Poverty Rates, 2005–2019	24
20	Per-Province Poverty Rates, 2005–2019	25
21	Multidimensional Poverty Head Count Ratios, 2015	25
22	Organizations Involved in Urban Planning in Pakistan	28
23	Relationship of Provincial Government Departments to Main City Functions	31
24	Population Using Safely Managed Water Services, 2000–2022	51

| 25 | Household Sanitation Systems, 2020 | 55 |
| 26 | Garbage Collection Coverage, 2018–2019 | 59 |

Boxes

| 1 | Lessons from Project Success and Failure in the Urban Sector of Pakistan | 72 |
| 2 | Summary of Proposed Action Points | 79 |

Acknowledgments

The Asian Development Bank (ADB) has supported the urban sector of Pakistan with sector analysis, policy development, and preliminary project assessments through technical assistance (TA). This national urban assessment, completed under the regional TA: Strengthening Urban Investment Planning and Capacity for Project Preparation and Implementation in Central and West Asia, aims to provide an overarching analytical framework and strategic context for integrated urban development in the country. It analyzes the urbanization process; identifies the leading environmental, social, and economic development issues relating to the urban sector; and examines potential ADB value addition and areas of support to make cities more livable, green, competitive, resilient, and inclusive, in line with ADB's Strategy 2030.

ADB would like to acknowledge with sincere appreciation the valuable support provided by the following federal and local development agencies of Pakistan: Ministry of Climate Change; National Disaster Risk Management Fund; Global Change Impact Studies Centre; Planning and Development Board, Punjab; Local Government and Community Development Department, Punjab; Housing, Urban Development and Public Health Engineering Department, Punjab; Urban Unit of Punjab; Public–Private Partnership Cell, Punjab; Punjab Mass Transit Authority; Environmental Protection Department, Punjab; Water And Sanitation Agency Lahore; Solid Waste Management Company Lahore; Metropolitan Corporation Lahore; Lahore Development Authority; Public–Partnership Unit, Sindh; Karachi Development Authority; Karachi Municipal Corporation; Quetta Development Authority; Peshawar Development Authority; Capital Development Authority; and Local Government, Elections and Rural Development Department of Khyber Pakhtunkhwa. Officials from these agencies participated in the extensive consultation process that helped define this national urban assessment's scope, validate research findings, and finalize this report. The consultations were undertaken mainly through digital means due to the coronavirus disease (COVID-19) pandemic.

ADB would also like to thank the country representatives and/or key managers of the Asian Infrastructure Investment Bank; French Development Agency, AFD; Deutsche Gesellschaft für Internationale Zusammenarbeit, GIZ; International Union for Conservation of Nature; United Nations Development Programme (UNDP); United Nations Children's Fund (UNICEF); and the World Bank for their valuable inputs. Furthermore, the project team is grateful to Yong Ye, Country Director, Pakistan Resident Mission (PRM), ADB; Jingmin Huang, Director, Water and Urban Development Sector Office (SG-WUD), Sectors Group, ADB; and Heeyoung Hong, Principal Urban Development Specialist, SG-WUD for providing overall guidance to the project. Finally, we would like to thank all ADB Staff and consultants in PRM and headquarters and publication professionals and artists who contributed to this report.

Project Team:
Xijie Lu, Urban Development Specialist, SG-WUD
Kiyoshi Nakamitsu, Principal Urban Development Specialist, SG-WUD
Mian S. Shafi, Unit Head, PRM
Syed Umar Ali Shah, Senior Project Officer, SG-WUD
Asif, Climate Change Officer, Climate Change and Sustainable Development Department

Consultants:
Spiro N. Pollalis, Professor of Design Technology and Management, Emeritus, Harvard Design School
Mark Ellery, Institutional Development Consultant
Syed Tahir Qadri, Climate Change and Risk Assessment Consultant
Dimosthenis Lappas, Urban Planning Consultant
Naeem Rehman, Team Liaison in Islamabad
Maira Khan, Urban Development Consultant
Maleeha Kiyani, Policy and Institutional Development Consultant

Technical Reviewers:
Benjamin Graham, Advisor, Independent Evaluation Department, ADB
Hong Soo Lee, Senior Urban Specialist (Smart Cities), SG-WUD
Peter Rowe, Professor of Architecture and Urban Design, Harvard University

Abbreviations

ADB	Asian Development Bank	PHED	public health engineering department
ADP	annual development plan or program	PMA	Punjab Masstransit Authority
BRT	bus rapid transit	PPP	public–private partnership
CDA	Capital Development Authority	PSDP	Public Sector Development Programme
COVID-19	coronavirus disease		
DISCO	distribution company (electricity)	SDG	Sustainable Development Goal
FY	fiscal year	SLGO	Sindh Local Government Ordinance
GDP	gross domestic product	SSWMB	Sindh Solid Waste Management Board
GHG	greenhouse gas	SWM	solid waste management
GLOF	glacial lake outburst flood	TFR	total fertility rate
km^2	square kilometer	UHI	urban heat island
KP	Khyber Pakhtunkhwa	UNDP	United Nations Development Programme
KWSB	Karachi Water and Sanitation Board		
KWSC	Karachi Water and Sewerage Corporation	UNICEF	United Nations Children's Fund
		WASA	water and sanitation agency
LGA	local government act	WHO	World Health Organization
LG&CD	local government and community development	WSSC	water and sanitation services company
		WWTP	wastewater treatment plant
LM&IS	Land Management and Infrastructure Wing (National Housing Authority)		
LWMC	Lahore Waste Management Company		
mgd	million gallons per day		
MPI	multidimensional poverty index		
MOCC&EC	Ministry of Climate Change and Environmental Coordination		
MTBF	Medium-Term Budgetary Framework		
NCCP	National Climate Change Policy		
NDC	nationally determined contribution		
O&M	operation and maintenance		
OPHI	Oxford Poverty and Human Development Initiatives		
P&D	planning and development		
PC	Planning Commission		
PDWP	Provincial Development Working Party		
PEFA	Public Expenditure and Financial Accountability		
PFM	public financial management		

Executive Summary

Urban Sector Overview

Demographics and Urbanization

Pakistan's population and urbanization challenges are increasing. Despite moderating in 2020 and 2021, Pakistan's population growth averaged 2.55% annually in 2017–2023. This was marked by a 3.65% annual growth in urban population, nearly double that of the rural population. This brought Pakistan's total population in 2023 to 241.5 million (16.3% more than in 2017), with an urban population of 93.8 million (approaching a fourfold increase since 1981). Recent projections place the country's population at over 400 million by 2050, with Pakistan one of only eight countries likely to account for more than half of the world population increases until 2050. The pressure on cities mired in ever-increasing deficits in urban infrastructure and services will intensify, with urban population projected to climb to 99.4 million, or 40.7% of the country's total, in 2030.

There are concerns that Pakistan's urban population has been underestimated. Since the 1981 census, Pakistan has defined urban and rural areas based on administrative boundaries, ignoring expansions and fast-growing peri-urban areas. This has resulted in a continued underestimation of the urban population. The unaccounted-for and hidden urbanization has impeded thorough analysis of the associated issues and due consideration of the opportunities arising from urbanization. Adjusting for this underestimation will allow urban development and planning to respond to the actual and emerging urbanization challenges.

Urbanization trends in Pakistan concentrate the demographic pressure in a few major cities. As Pakistan's urbanization escalated so has the trend toward the concentration of the urban population in the larger urban centers. By 2017, 54% of the country's urban dwellers lived in just 21 major urban localities with populations exceeding 500,000, with 34.5% of them in the megacities of Karachi and Lahore. In each of the provinces, the capital cities hold a disproportionately large share of the provincial urban population, concentrating both the political and administrative pressures of urbanization.

Planning and managing urbanization are critical for Pakistan to optimize socioeconomic development. The high-speed growth of Pakistan's urban population has led to a commensurate and hazardous urban sprawl. The growth of illegal developments and informal settlements that do not comply with planning rules or building codes delivers substandard living conditions, disrupts city functions, and degrades the urban environment. The associated encroachment into agricultural lands erodes future food security. With these mounting challenges of urbanization, Pakistan needs to direct greater policy, planning, and investment support to transform its cities into safe, resilient, and livable spaces, as well as economic powerhouses that provide better income, education, and livelihood opportunities.

Economic Environment

Pakistan's rapid urbanization is occurring in an uncertain economic environment. Even before the coronavirus disease pandemic, Pakistan's economy was in a steep decline, characteristic of its boom-and-bust cycle. By the end of fiscal year (FY) 2022, Pakistan's trade and fiscal deficits ballooned, while inflation rose to double-digit levels due to the sizable depreciation of the Pakistan rupee, upward fuel and electricity price adjustments, and global inflationary pressures from geopolitical tensions. An acute foreign reserves shortage, massive damages and economic losses from floods, and ongoing political instability constrained the economy in FY2023. As a result, gross domestic product (GDP) growth plummeted, and headline inflation rose to the country's highest in the last 5 decades to 2023.

Implementation of the economic adjustment program is crucial for restoring macroeconomic stability and economic growth. Pakistan's GDP growth is projected to recover modestly to 1.9% in FY2024, with inflation easing to 25% amid significant downside risks, including global price shocks and slower global growth. These near-term growth prospects are closely tied to the successful implementation of the economic adjustment program supported by the International Monetary Fund and other bilateral and multilateral development partners. With a focus on fiscal discipline, a market-determined exchange rate, reforms in the energy sector and state-owned enterprises, expanded social and development spending, and related governance and institutional reforms, the economic adjustment program aims to stabilize the economy and rebuild fiscal and external buffers.

The rising dominance of the industry and services sectors in Pakistan's major cities fuels the engines of economic development. While agriculture remains the biggest source of employment at the national level, services, followed by industry, are the biggest sources of employment in all major cities. In 2018, the cities generated 55% of the country's GDP, with the 10 major cities accounting for 95% of the federal tax revenue. Karachi alone contributed 12%–15% of the national GDP and 55% of the federal tax revenue in 2018.

Urban Governance

The institutional framework for urban governance has been complicated by partial devolution. In 2010, the 18th Amendment to the Constitution of Pakistan mandated the devolution of powers from the federal to the provincial governments and required the provinces to further devolve fiscal, political, and administrative authority to the local governments through Article 140-A. Partial implementation of provincial local government acts (LGAs) has given rise to a complex urban governance model, characterized by the involvement of multiple stakeholders in urban planning, land management, and municipal services, with unclear mandates, overlapping functions, and competing interests. In the absence of the transfer of adequate funds or functionaries to local governments, the devolution of functions has created a system where neither the provinces nor local governments can deliver and efficiently manage urban services.

Multiple mutually exclusive governance structures militate against the clear assignment of liability for municipal service failures. The accountability of multiple municipal service providers that operate within urban jurisdictions is not necessarily linked to the responsible local government. This includes the local development authorities (responsible for land use planning and management), water and sanitation agencies (responsible for the provision of networked water and sewage services), traffic engineering and planning agencies (responsible for developing transport infrastructure), cantonment boards (responsible for the local provision of municipal services on military-owned establishments), and industrial estates and private housing societies (responsible for local housing developments and their management). In the absence of any agreement delegating responsibility from the local government to these municipal service providers, elected urban local governments cannot coordinate these providers to ensure a minimum quality of municipal services for all their citizens.

The differing approaches to devolution by provinces will impact urbanization. Varied provincial amendments to the LGAs establishing different urban–rural interfaces present an opportunity to learn how these different structures affect urbanization. For example, the 2019 amendments to the LGA of Khyber Pakhtunkhwa (KP) abolished the district councils, creating a single two-tier governance structure of urban and rural municipal councils at the subdistrict level, potentially more adept at managing the urban–rural interface. On the other hand, the Punjab LGA 2022 abolished the subdistrict councils, creating two parallel urban and rural two-tier local government structures, potentially retaining greater capacity within their district municipal services providers. Though still in their early implementation stages, the impact of these initiatives on municipal service delivery can inform decision-making on urban governance.

Urban Planning

The absence of a nationally informed approach to urbanization has resulted in a patchwork of trial-and-error approaches. In the wake of the 18th Constitutional Amendment, the national urban policy formulated in 2011 was never implemented by the provincial and local governments. Although most provinces have developed urban-related policies and/or strategies, the absence of any system for sharing learning on urbanization among the provinces fails to build on the precious lessons learned.

Urban planning processes have continued to evolve despite weak compliance. Comprehensive urban planning commenced in Pakistan with the preparation of the Greater Lahore Master Plan in 1961–1966. Between 1960 and 1980, urban planning primarily focused on land use planning, leading to the preparation of master plans, land use plans, and zoning plans. From 1980 to 2000, the approach shifted toward the drafting of long-term, policy-driven vision documents like outline development plans and structure plans. In 2001, the term "spatial plan" was widely used to refer to various urban planning documents. The promulgation of Punjab Land Use Rules 2009 gave impetus to the preparation of peri-urban and land use classification and/or reclassification plans. This marked a shift in focus from already developed urban areas to rapidly urbanizing peri-urban areas, resulting in significant land use changes. Despite the evolution of urban planning practices, the sheer complexity of approval procedures required for development planning has resulted in a lack of compliance with plans at local levels.

Municipal and district local governments are responsible for urban planning, land development, and municipal service delivery. The responsibility for the registration and/or acquisition of land resides with provincial governments; however, provinces have variously delegated the responsibility for the approval of spatial, zoning, and land use plans, and their enforcement, subject to an approved master plan, to the municipal or district local governments. In the absence of a master plan in urban or rural areas, the municipal and district local governments are empowered to establish their own land use plans and regulate land development approvals through the passage of local bylaws and regulations. Although rarely practiced, this does enable rural local governments to implement urban land use plans and development approval processes within their urbanizing rural areas.

Several local development authorities are responsible for urban planning and development. In larger cities where local development authorities have been established, they are responsible for the preparation of master plans and the implementation and regulation of spatial, zoning, and land use plans. While the LGAs envisage that the local development authorities will operate as a ring-fenced entity while under the delegated authority of the municipal local government, the reality is that these local development authorities are neither bound by a service agreement with the municipal local government nor immune from political influence.

Urban units can offer much-needed capacity for urban planning. In recognition of the multisectoral capacity requirements for the preparation of master plans, different provinces have either established independent or in-house urban units or a combination of both. There is, however, still room for improvement. While the LGAs envisage that the preparation and approval of a master plan by an independent urban unit will be accountable to the municipal and district local governments (in some cases, through local development authorities), this is rarely the case. On the other hand, while the master plans prepared by provincial urban units tend to be more successful in securing funding from provincial departments for public infrastructure, the commitment of the municipal and district local governments to the execution of provincially developed master plans is limited.

Municipal Finances

Inadequate finance is a significant obstacle facing Pakistani cities. The own-source revenue assignment to municipal local governments is meager. They are authorized to collect only minor taxes and fees (e.g., parking, entertainment, licenses and permits, and property rentals), which they use to defray their operational costs. Sales and property taxes are collected by the provincial governments, while all other major taxes (e.g., personal and corporate income taxes, which constitute the bulk of tax revenues) are collected by the federal government. Consequently, urban authorities have limited finances and rely on budgetary provisions from their provincial government to improve local infrastructure and deliver essential services. This long-standing reliance on provincial allocations has reinforced the patron–client tradition in local governance and disincentivized the municipalities from delivering services in a manner that simultaneously increases their own financial capacity and revenue base.

Poor cost-recovery by publicly owned utilities has increased the reliance on government subsidies, resulting in a build–neglect–rebuild cycle of service delivery. The consistently low own-source revenues generated by public utilities have decreased their accountability to customers for the delivery of high-quality public services, while their high reliance on government subsidies has increased their accountability to the provincial governments for the provision of public infrastructure. The resulting build–neglect–rebuild cycle of service delivery not only results in a low quality of service at a high cost but also undermines the financial viability of utilities and their capacity to expand services to meet the demands of rapid urbanization. Innovations are desperately needed to break through the unwillingness of governments to charge and of customers to pay for the full cost of services currently received to enable utilities to extend high-quality municipal services to all urban residents.

Climate Assessment

The increasing frequency and intensity of extreme weather events are indicative of escalating climate risks. Pakistan ranked eighth among countries most affected by extreme weather events in 2000–2019, and in July–August 2022, suffered one of the worst floods in its history. Moreover, in what may foreshadow the more frequent alternating of extreme weather events, these floods were preceded by a severe heat wave. The increased severity of droughts in the arid areas of Balochistan and Sindh prompted the Government of Sindh to declare southern parts of the province calamity areas in 2018.

The costs of climate-related disasters to Pakistan are substantial and rising. The estimated $30 billion total economic cost of the 2022 floods surpassed the $10 billion cost of the 2010 floods. It equated to an 8% GDP loss in 2022, with spillover effects amounting to a 2.2% GDP decline in 2023. The 2010 and 2022 floods killed a total of more than 3,700 people, while the livelihoods of millions were lost due to massive crop damage. In 2015, the deadliest heat wave in Pakistan's history killed some 1,200 people in Karachi alone. Looking ahead, a 2022 United Nations study has indicated that Pakistan will have the highest projected GDP loss from climate change in the South Asia and Southwest Asia regions, reaching 9.1% annually under the worst-case climate scenario.

The link between urbanization and climate change is deep and multifaceted. Cities are at the forefront of climate change. They account for 75% of global carbon emissions, are the main agents of land use change, and produce high levels of pollution that could aggravate temperature increases. They are also susceptible to peculiar climate change impacts such as the urban heat island effect and are likely to bear the brunt of climate- and disaster-related impacts due to their concentration of people and assets. Given these intricate and inextricable links, all countries must integrate climate change adaptation and mitigation in urban planning and management.

Pakistan is committed to climate change mitigation and adaptation. In its 2021 update to its nationally determined contributions under the Paris Agreement, Pakistan raised its emissions reduction target from 20% in 2016 to 50% of its projected 2030 emissions. With the National Adaptation Plan in place, adaptation efforts will systematically seek to address priority areas of concern, such as the agriculture–water nexus, natural capital, urban resilience, and human capital. Existing federal programs in the urban sector, including the Clean Green Pakistan and Recharge Pakistan, will be expanded. A range of actions reducing the urban contribution to energy, industry, transport, and agriculture-related emissions have also been proposed.

Urban Needs

Housing

Housing in cities has not kept pace with rapid urban population growth. The average annual supply of 150,000 new urban housing units falls well short of the demand for 350,000 new housing units per year. This deficit, amounting to nearly 10 million housing units in 2018, has led to 57% of urban residents living in informal settlements. The typically overcrowded and squalid conditions for those in informal settlements contrast sharply with those in the new, single-family housing schemes in suburban areas and the exclusive, gated communities in the city centers. The double dilemma is that the green and open spaces, rights-of-way of railroads, traffic arteries, ravines, and riverbanks occupied by informal settlements disrupt the functioning of cities, increase their vulnerability to flooding, and degrade the environment for all urban residents.

The availability of land and housing is constrained by political economy considerations. This is a result of multiple factors that restrict the availability of land for development and deprive low-income groups of access to affordable housing. It has been driven by (i) the politician–developer nexus, which has facilitated the rise of exclusive gated communities fostering segregation, inequality, and insecurity; (ii) the co-optation of housing programs meant for low-income groups by private interests; and (iii) the use of state taxation to shelter private land interests.

The messy urbanization model is sustained by lucrative market forces. The profits from open plot development projects in rural areas and the associated incomes that accrue to municipal governments or development authorities have become a springboard for speculative land investment schemes. While the government objective in property development markets should be to guarantee access to high-quality municipal services for prospective residents while transferring the maximum viable costs and risks to private developers, it is also true that the more lucrative the profits of property development, the more space there is for speculative public offerings and private investments. Given the flourishing market for property developers, local governments have an opportunity to transfer more responsibilities for municipal service development (e.g., roads, pavements, stormwater drains, water and sewerage, and electricity) and property development (e.g., solar panels, low wattage lights, groundwater recharge, and passive thermal design) to property developers in the public release of land, the classification of land for development, or the approval of development applications.

Water and Sanitation

Pakistan is highly water-stressed. In 2015, the World Resources Institute projected that Pakistan would rank 23rd among the 33 countries facing very high water stress levels by 2040. Amid increasing temperatures, rapid population growth, and low water storage capacity, the country was already highly water-stressed in 2015, extracting 74.3% of its freshwater resources annually, according to the United Nations Development Programme (UNDP).

Despite the looming water crisis, access to water supply and sanitation services has improved. However, the improvements have been incremental, and huge deficits remain. As of 2022, some 39 million or 43% of the urban population did not have access to a safely managed water service, while an estimated 15.7 million or 18% of urban dwellers lacked access to a basic sanitation service. The water supply in cities has remained inadequate and irregular, meeting only around half of the demand and lasting only a few hours a day and/or a few days a week, with most of the underserved groups residing in informal settlements and on the periphery of cities.

Several factors other than diminishing water resources underlie severe urban water shortages. These factors include aging infrastructure, lack of proper maintenance, and weak sector governance and capacities. In Karachi, it is estimated that 35%–58% of the treated water supply is lost due to water theft, leakages, and an outdated water distribution system. In cities across Punjab and Balochistan, localized depletion of the groundwater table and high nonrevenue water losses have made water supply too costly for some small and intermediate cities. Across KP, water supplies in urban areas are limited by inadequate storage capacity, unreliable power supplies, and significant water distribution losses.

The safe containment, transport, treatment, and disposal of wastewater is a pernicious problem. Frequently, wastewater from toilets discharges into open drains, sewage lines are blocked and bypassed, and treatment plants are nonexistent or fail to adequately treat the wastewater. As a result, most of the municipal and industrial wastewater in Pakistan is discharged untreated into the receiving environment—aggravating air, water, and soil pollution; contaminating water supply sources; and harming the aquatic and marine ecosystems.

Drainage

The increasing imperviousness of urban surfaces is a major factor behind urban flooding. This imperviousness is due to the loss of green cover and soil sealing that comes with massive construction work and infrastructure development. Urban flooding is exacerbated, furthermore, by aging and overburdened drainage systems, a lack of rainwater storage and management systems, inadequate waste disposal systems, institutional capacity constraints, weak urban governance, and development that ignores topography and landscape.

Solid Waste Management

While access has improved, solid waste management services have remained limited and inefficient. Although 67% of the population reported no garbage collection system in 2019–2020, this is a noticeable improvement from the 76% without access in 2013–2014. However, this still means that two-thirds of the population resorts to open dumping and/or burning of their waste. In most cities in Pakistan, there is no waste segregation, no recycling, no waste reduction program at source, and no comprehensive solid waste management (SWM) strategy. Citizen awareness of proper waste disposal is low, with most collected waste ending up in uncontrolled, unsanitary landfills.

Private sector participation has improved solid waste management. In Lahore, the engagement of two foreign operators for waste collection significantly reduced the accumulation of waste in the city. The situation is the same in three of Karachi's six districts where SWM has been outsourced to private contractors. Despite some initial deterioration when Lahore shifted to local private operators, the experience with outsourcing SWM to the private sector has been positive in both cities.

Urban Development Futures

Pakistan requires a new urbanization model. The economic and social benefits of urban agglomeration in Pakistan are being undermined by failing public services, declining quality of life, and flagging economic productivity. The current urban development model perpetuates these challenges and needs to be replaced by a sustainable urbanization model. This new urbanization model should (i) seek to internalize the economic, environmental, and social benefits associated with higher levels of agglomeration; (ii) be fueled by robust planning and evaluation capacities that extend vertically (clearly demarcating governance responsibilities) and horizontally (internalizing multisector service requirements), as well as spatially (optimizing land use) and temporally (investing financially in development needs); and (iii) be steered by proactive institutions that underwrite the social and economic well-being of urban citizens with the public services and infrastructure necessary to sustain growth without detrimental social and environmental consequences. This requires progressive reforms in urban governance and a proactive urban planning framework to replace the current reactive approach to urbanization.

Urban Governance

Provincial governments must bridge the gap between local government acts and their implementation. The various provincial local government acts (LGAs) have mandated the transfer of responsibility for municipal service provision to local governments while retaining the responsibility of policy-making with provincial governments. To date, provinces have made little progress in relinquishing control over the funds or the functionaries that deliver municipal services in urban areas. This absence of local government capacity has resulted in a lack of coordination among municipal service providers. The LGAs have also authorized urban and rural local governments to pass bylaws to approve and/or implement land use and spatial plans (including the classification and reclassification of land) and approve or reject land development proposals. The absence of local government capacity to oversee land development plans has given rise to uncontrolled urbanization.

A vertically and horizontally delineated urban governance model is consistent with existing legislation. Existing LGAs tend to separate the regulation of failure (by provincial governments), the licensing of compliance (by local governments), the delivery of services (by public and private operators), and the arbitration of disputes (by commissions). Under this LGA structure (i) the provincial government is responsible for establishing the laws, policies, regulations, and standards for all urban development subsectors (e.g., water supply, sewerage and sanitation, waste management, and mobility) and regulating failure through oversight, spot checks, and clear-cut reporting and accountability systems; (ii) the local government is responsible for the licensing or contracting of urban service providers (public or private; locally, provincially, or federally owned) and ensuring compliance with provincial laws and pieces of legislation; (iii) the service providers are responsible for generating revenues from their customers, investing in service improvements, and returning any dividend to the utility owners; and (iv) the independent commissions for local government, local government finance, and elections are responsible for arbitrating on the means to resolve the disconnect between legislation and practice. Closer adherence to and actual implementation of the provisions of the LGAs should reduce the inefficiencies and fragmentation that stem from the multiplicity of agencies in urban development with unclear mandates and overlapping functions.

Sustainable Urban Planning

Forward-looking urban planning needs to integrate solutions to the known challenges of urbanization. This requires a multisectoral planning approach that fosters the allocation of land, capital, and labor across conventional boundaries to maximize the social, environmental, and economic returns for all. It also requires the progressive reinterpretation of urban spaces to reduce the negative externalities of one sector on another (e.g., housing, energy, transport, water, health, education, recreation, social services, and environment). Such a holistic planning approach will enable cities to develop synergies and complementarities across sectors to capture the most benefits for all. The appropriate deployment of urban units with multisectoral technical competency can continue to facilitate this shift to an integrated urban planning approach.

Urban planning should channel the increasing value of land toward the provision of public services. Coupled with efforts to distribute service costs to beneficiaries through user fees (e.g., road tolls and metered water), increasing public revenues from the development of urban land should lead to the continued enhancement and expansion of services and incremental increase in revenue sources. By linking service liabilities to the investments made by urban service providers and by mandating social and environmental provisions in property developments, ongoing budget pressures on local governments should gradually ease. The easing of budget pressure from current liabilities should enable municipalities to shift toward strategic budgeting of plans that deliver higher social, economic, and environmental benefits.

Land use allocations need to guide rather than chase messy urbanization. The allocations of land and the approval of developments needs to be progressively redefined to enable public infrastructure to guide planned urbanization rather than chase messy urbanization. This can build on existing LGA provisions, empowering local governments to approve land use plans and exercise control over development proposals. It implies the need for (i) regular assessments of urbanization trends (e.g., increases in housing and transport densities, decreases in green spaces, and evolution of business areas) to inform land use approval requirements with development imperatives and opportunities that evolve; and (ii) the staging of development planning (i.e., the process of dividing large-scale development projects into smaller, more manageable stages) to outline the division of responsibilities (whether municipality or developer) in the provision of public, environmental, and social services in accordance with local bylaws, zoning regulations, and the nature of the development. Coordination in the development of multisectoral urban master plans, along with routine reviews of the execution of these plans, should strengthen both compliance and timely updating.

Mixed-use, pedestrian-friendly, vertical urbanization is more likely to be sustainable. Overarching land use and master planning frameworks in Pakistan should prioritize increased vertical mixed-use developments and pedestrian-friendly urban areas. It should foster the creation of public and community spaces while also accommodating a broad range of urban activities that are commercial, cultural, environmental, and educational. It should also incentivize investments in high-rise, inner-city regeneration projects or the vertical redevelopment of informal settlements, reinforced with policies for property developers to invest in affordable housing, energy efficiency, and green spaces.

Urban Development Scenarios

Short Term (1 to 10 years)

Strengthen municipal authorities to approve and enforce risk-informed development plans and license out urban services; strengthen local government capacity for increasing own-source revenue, gender-responsive budgeting and expenditure, and strengthening operation and maintenance systems; update existing urban master plans as risk-informed urban master plans requiring routine compliance or revisions; institutionalize a culture of accountability in local, provincial, and federal governments; pilot public–private partnership agreements defining municipal service delivery standards; strengthen provincial departmental capacity to identify service delivery failures; enhance financial sustainability through cost-recovery mechanisms among service providers; and launch an urban regeneration project centered on high-density and mixed-use development.

Medium Term (10 to 20 years)

Scale up commercially viable public–private partnership agreements for the delivery of different municipal services; expand the high-density regeneration model across cities with private sector involvement; scale up e-governance and smart city applications; and enhance the independence and capacity of local government commissions.

Long Term (20 to 30 years)

Create competitive, resilient, and sustainable urban centers; foster economic, social, and cultural activities in regenerated urban centers; embed circular economy principles in planning and development; and leverage demographic dividends and empower women in economically competitive urban centers.

Urban Sector Overview

Demographics and Urbanization

Pakistan is a federation divided administratively into the provinces of Balochistan, Khyber Pakhtunkhwa (KP), Punjab, and Sindh; and the northern regions. Islamabad, the country's capital, is federally administered and constitutes the Islamabad Capital Territory. The provinces and regions are subdivided into divisions and further into three administrative tiers: (a) districts, (b) *tehsils* (subdistricts), and (c) union councils.

The four provinces and the northern regions have similar systems of government. The provincial government consists of a directly elected provincial assembly, which elects a chief minister who appoints and oversees a cabinet of ministers. In 2010, the 18th Amendment to the Constitution strengthened the jurisdiction of provincial governments on urban affairs.[1] However, there are significant geographical, demographic, economic, and social differences among the provinces and regions that affect the urban fabric and the degree to which cities embrace or undertake reforms.

Population Size and Growth Rate

The 2023 digital census placed the country's population at 241.5 million, up by 33.8 million or 16.3% from the preceding 2017 census.[2] It is projected to reach 403 million by 2050,[3] with Pakistan among the eight countries likely to account for more than half of the world population increases until 2050.[4]

The average annual population growth rate over 2017–2023 was 2.55% (footnote 2), representing the first time the country's population grew faster than the previous intercensal period. Pakistan's average annual population growth rate stood at 2.4% in 1998–2017, down from 2.7% in 1981–1998, 3.1% in 1972–1981, and 3.6% in 1961–1972.[5] The latest census increase also contrasts with the recent global trend of slower population growth that, for the first time since 1950, dropped to below 1% in 2020 (footnote 4).

---

[1] Senate Secretariat. 2010. Constitution (Eighteenth Amendment) Act, 2010. *The Gazette of Pakistan*. 20 April.
[2] Pakistan Bureau of Statistics. 2023. Announcement of Results of 7th Population and Housing Census-2023 'The Digital Census'. Final Results: Pakistan.
[3] United Nations Fund for Population Activities (UNFPA). 2023. *8 Billion Lives, Infinite Possibilities: The Case for Rights and Choices. State of World Population 2023*.
[4] United Nations, Department of Economic and Social Affairs. Population Division. 2022. *World Population Prospects 2022: Summary of Results*.
[5] Government of Pakistan, Ministry of Planning, Development and Special Initiatives. Pakistan Bureau of Statistics. Undated. *Pakistan National Census Report 2017*.

Provincial and Local Ramifications

Provincial populations have expanded significantly since 1998 (Figure 1). Until mid-2023, Punjab was the most populous province, with more than half of the national population; Balochistan, the least populated, comprised around a 6% share.

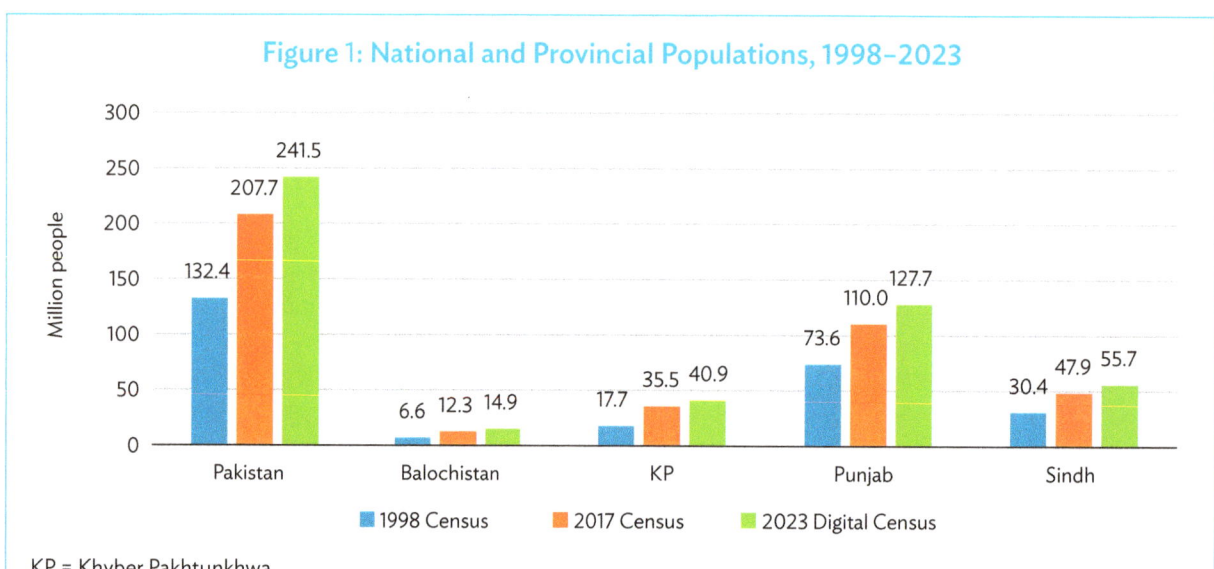

Figure 1: National and Provincial Populations, 1998–2023

KP = Khyber Pakhtunkhwa.
Notes:
1. The 1998 census covered 1981–1998; the 2017 census covered 1998–2017; and the 2023 digital census covered 2017–2023.
2. In the 1998 census, KP was still named North West Frontier Province.
3. The 2017 population data of KP in Table 1 Final Results (Census–2023) includes that of the Federally Administered Tribal Areas, which were merged with KP in 2018. This explains the discrepancy in the 2017 population data of KP in the two reference tables.

Sources: Pakistan Bureau of Statistics. Table–1 Final Results (Census–2017) and Table 1 Final Results (Census–2023).

While similarly registering net increases, the average annual growth rate of provincial populations followed opposite trajectories over the past three intercensal periods. After declining in 1998–2017 from their 1981–1998 levels, the growth rates of Punjab and Sindh rose in 2017–2023, while those of KP and Balochistan increased in 1998–2017 and fell in 2017–2023 (Figure 2). The contrasting patterns could reflect the varying ways and extent fertility rate and migration, the two key factors behind Pakistan's population changes, have played into the local population dynamics. For instance, although internal migration played a role, the increases in the previous intercensal period were overall driven by a sluggish decrease in the total fertility rate (TFR), which fell only by around 0.5 births per woman between 2005 and 2017.[6] TFR varied among the provinces: in 2017, it was 4.0 in Balochistan and KP, 3.6 in Sindh, and 3.4 in Punjab.

Becoming largely an intra-provincial phenomenon, internal migration in 1998–2017, on the other hand, was highest in Punjab at 13.4%, followed by Sindh with 8.0%, KP with 6.7%, and Balochistan with 6.1%. Most districts and subdistricts in all provinces also saw their populations rising at generally higher rates in urban areas.[7]

---

[6] G.M. Arif. 2019. Population Growth: Implications for Human Development. *Development Advocate Pakistan*. (6) 1. pp. 15–17.
[7] Pakistan Bureau of Statistics. Final Results (Census–2017). District and *Tehsil* Tables (accessed 10 May 2023).

However, the provinces saw some shifts in migration patterns in subsequent years. By 2020, Balochistan registered the highest migration rate at 12%—6% intra-province and 6% inter-province; Punjab followed at 7%—6% intra-province and 1% inter-province; Sindh was next at 6%—3% intra-province and 3% inter-province; and KP was last with a 4% migration rate—all intra-provincial.[8] This may partly explain the latest decrease in Balochistan's population growth rate. Meanwhile, Pakistan's TFR declined sharply, from 3.8 in 2017 to 3.5 in 2021, compared to the world average of 2.5 in 2017 and 2.3 in 2021.[9]

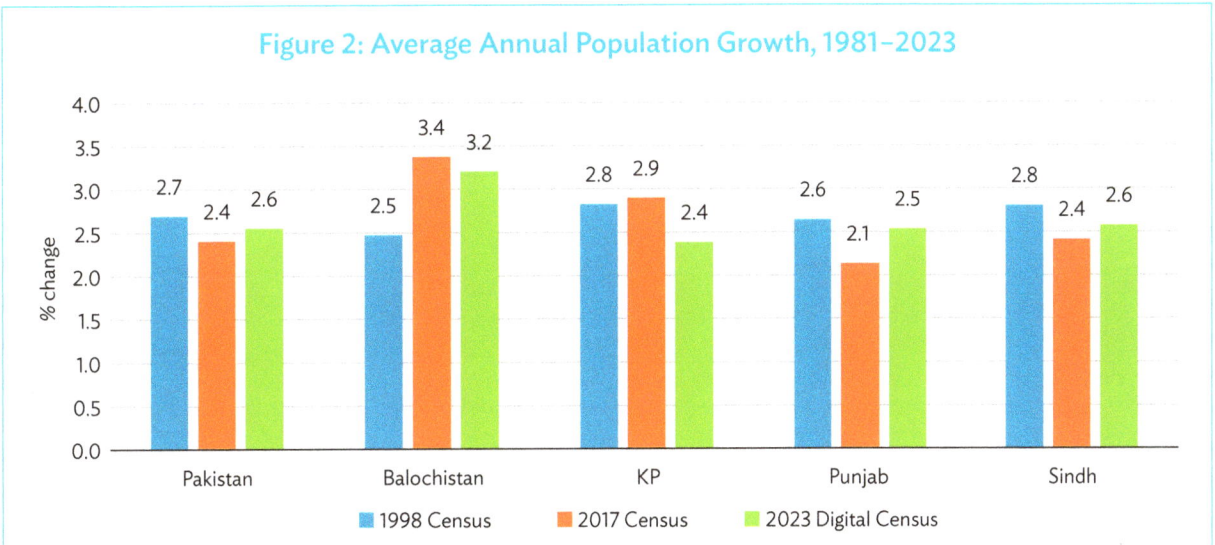

Figure 2: Average Annual Population Growth, 1981–2023

KP = Khyber Pakhtunkhwa.

Notes:
1. The 1998 census covered 1981–1998; the 2017 census covered 1998–2017; and the 2023 digital census covered 2017–2023.
2. In the 1998 census, KP was still named North West Frontier Province.
3. The 2017 annual population growth rate of KP in Table 1 Final Results (Census–2023) includes that of the Federally Administered Tribal Areas, which were merged with KP in 2018. This explains the discrepancy in the 2017 population data of KP in the two reference tables.

Sources: Pakistan Bureau of Statistics. Table–1 Final Results (Census–2017) and Table 1 Final Results (Census–2023) 'The Digital Census'.

Population Density

The population increases have caused population densities to soar, nationally and provincially (Figure 3). Notwithstanding this, Balochistan with large arid deserts remains sparsely populated. In contrast, Punjab with mostly fertile plains has over 14 times the population density of Balochistan.

Even with 536 persons/square kilometer (km^2) in 2017, Punjab already stood out as one of the most heavily populated regions in the world. Excluding microstates, it ranked third in population density, behind Lebanon with 597 persons/km^2 and Bangladesh with 1,243 persons/km^2. Lebanon's population density dropped to 554 persons/km^2 while that of Bangladesh climbed to 1,286 persons/km^2 in 2020.[10]

---

[8] Government of Pakistan, Ministry of Planning, Development and Special Initiatives. Pakistan Bureau of Statistics. 2021. *PSLM 2019–20. Pakistan Social and Living Standards Measurement Survey (2019–20)*.
[9] World Bank. Data. *Fertility Rate, Total (Births per Woman) – Pakistan* (accessed 10 May 2023).
[10] World Bank. Data. *Population Density (People per sq. km of Land Area)* (accessed 27 August 2023).

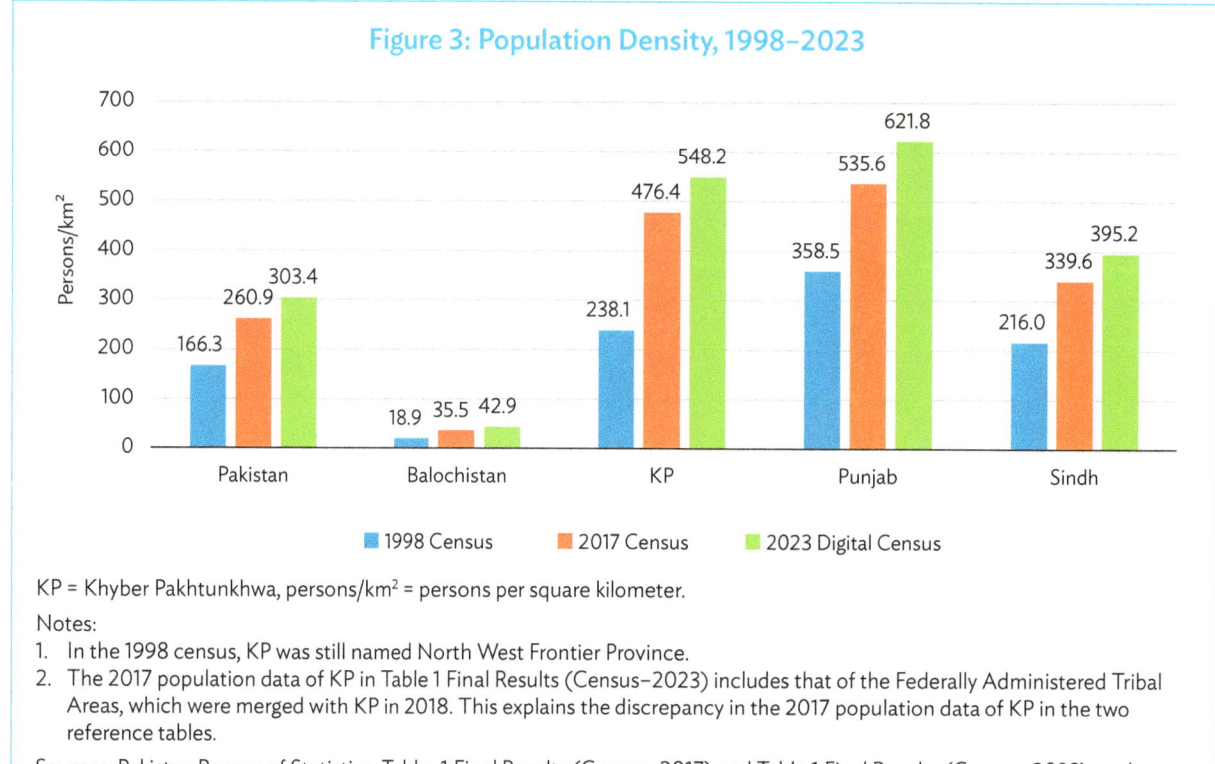

KP = Khyber Pakhtunkhwa, persons/km² = persons per square kilometer.
Notes:
1. In the 1998 census, KP was still named North West Frontier Province.
2. The 2017 population data of KP in Table 1 Final Results (Census–2023) includes that of the Federally Administered Tribal Areas, which were merged with KP in 2018. This explains the discrepancy in the 2017 population data of KP in the two reference tables.

Sources: Pakistan Bureau of Statistics. Table–1 Final Results (Census–2017) and Table 1 Final Results (Census–2023); and Government of Pakistan, Finance Division. *Pakistan Economic Survey 2021-22*.

Among the cities, Karachi has consistently topped the list. The city encompasses two of Pakistan's most densely populated districts, Karachi East and Karachi Central, and two of the world's most overpopulated residential areas, the Garden and Lyari subdivisions in Karachi South. In 2017, Karachi Central had 43,064 inhabitants/km², while similarly sized and high-rise Manhattan had 27,757 persons/km². By mid-2023, Manhattan's population density was estimated at 28,016/km²,[11] still far below that of Karachi Central in 2017. The Garden's population reached 99,273/km² and Lyari's was 103,082/km².

Wide disparities in population distribution and density within the provinces and across the cities have become increasingly conspicuous and challenging with the concentration of demographic pressures on a few urban areas. By 2017, these disparities became remarkable in the highly varying sizes and shares of the provinces' largest cities in the national, provincial, and urban populations (Table 1). They also showed up in wide-ranging district- and *tehsil*-level population densities and urban proportions within each province (footnote 7).

---

[11] World Population Review. *Manhattan Population 2023* (accessed 27 August 2023).

Table 1: Share of Each Province's Largest City in National, Provincial, and Urban Populations, 2017

City (Province)	Population Size	Share in Total Population %		Share in Urban Population %	
		National	Provincial	National	Provincial
Quetta (Balochistan)	907,925[a]	0.4	7.4	1.2	26.7
Peshawar (KP)	1,893,344[b]	0.9	6.2	2.5	33.0
Lahore (Punjab)	11,119,985[c]	5.4	10.1	14.7	27.4
Karachi (Sindh)	14,884,402[d]	7.2	31.1	19.7	59.9

KP = Khyber Pakhtunkhwa.
Note: Except for Lahore, no corresponding data are yet available from the 2023 digital census. The 2023 census placed the population of Lahore district at about 13 million.
[a] Quetta Metropolitan Corporation.
[b] Peshawar Municipal Corporation.
[c] Entire Lahore district.
[d] Entire urban population of Karachi division.
Source: Pakistan Bureau of Statistics. Final Results (Census–2017). Table–1: Pakistan and Table–2: Balochistan, Khyber Pakhtunkhwa, Punjab, and Sindh.

Age and Sex Composition

Updates from the Pakistan Demographic Survey–2020 have revealed (i) a drop in both the male and female population aged under 15 years old; (ii) an increase in both sexes in the working-age group, aged 15–64 years; and (iii) an increase in both sexes in the population aged 65 years and above (Figure 4).[12] The resulting net decline in the dependent-age groups (population aged under 15 years and 65 and above) and rise in the working-age group is a continuance of a demographic transition that started in Pakistan in the early 1990s but has remained largely economically untapped.[13] From 53.62% in 2000, the working-age group rose to 59.16% of the country's population in 2022, which, along with a consistent decline in the fertility rate, led to a decrease in the age-dependency ratio from 86.5% to 69.0% during 2000–2022.[14]

Given its current economic circumstances, Pakistan needs to maximize the opportunity to achieve a demographic dividend from its current population structure.[15] By integrating women and youth, who compose the bulk of its working-age population, into the economic mainstream, the country will also be able to address some of its prevailing social inequities and accelerate the progress of its poverty reduction agenda.

The case for directing greater policy and investment support toward improving the economic participation of women, whose ratio to men moved closer to 1:1 in the recent Pakistan Demographic Survey (footnote 12), becomes even stronger considering how it can contribute to decreasing the fertility rate. In Bangladesh, for example, the desire for large families was reduced by the increased opportunity cost of having children, which came with women's higher labor force participation (footnote 6).

---

[12] Government of Pakistan, Ministry of Planning, Development and Special Initiatives. Pakistan Bureau of Statistics. 2022. *Pakistan Demographic Survey—2020*.
[13] D. Nayab, R. Ul-Haq, and S. Bashir. 2019. The Dynamics of Population in Pakistan. *Development Advocate Pakistan*. (6) 1. pp. 2–9.
[14] Asian Development Bank. Key Indicators Database (accessed 12 August 2023).
[15] A demographic dividend "is the potential economic benefits offered by changes in the age structure of the population, during the demographic transition, when there is an increase in working age population and an associated decline in the dependent age population." Footnote 13, p. 3.

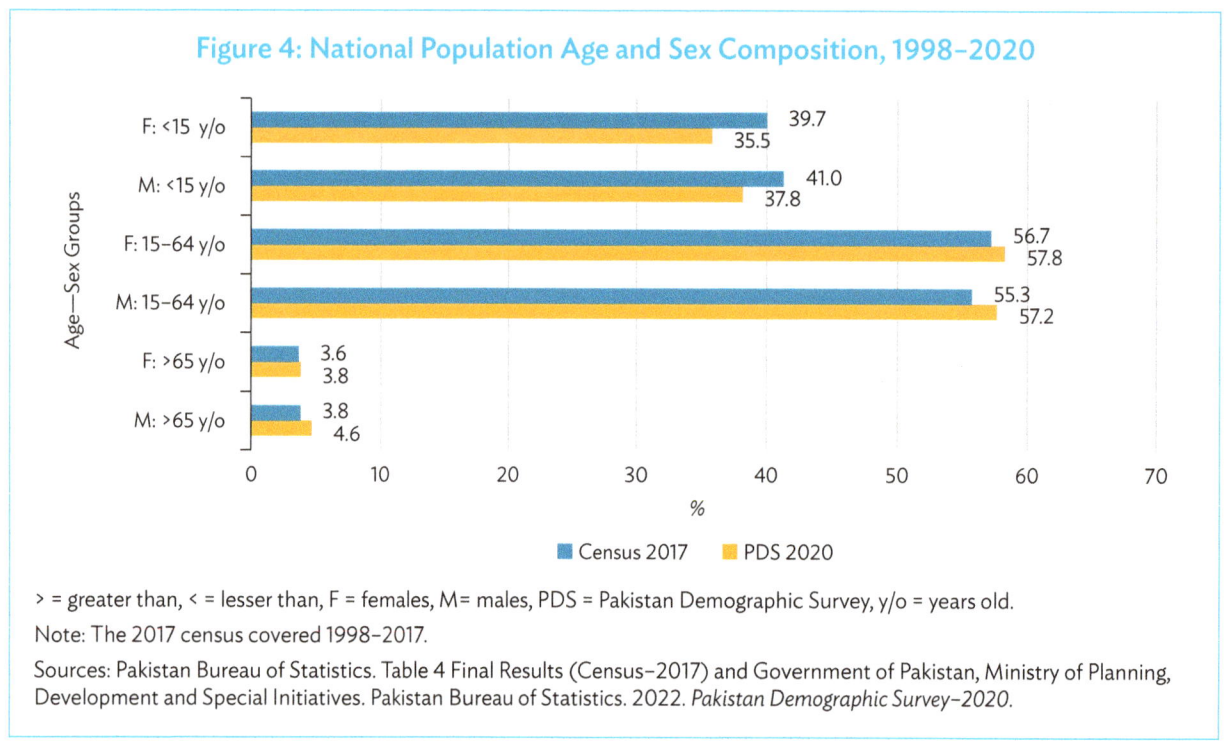

> = greater than, < = lesser than, F = females, M= males, PDS = Pakistan Demographic Survey, y/o = years old.
Note: The 2017 census covered 1998–2017.
Sources: Pakistan Bureau of Statistics. Table 4 Final Results (Census–2017) and Government of Pakistan, Ministry of Planning, Development and Special Initiatives. Pakistan Bureau of Statistics. 2022. *Pakistan Demographic Survey–2020*.

Urbanization Patterns

Pakistan's urban population rose almost fourfold in the 4 decades to 2023, reaching 93.8 million (footnote 2) from 23.8 million in 1981.[16] However, there are concerns that the urban population is underestimated.[17] Since the 1981 census, the government has delineated urban from rural areas based on administrative boundaries, ignoring expansions and fast-growing peri-urban areas. The definition should be amended to include functional and density-based factors that capture the dynamics and complexity of the ongoing urbanization process.

Nevertheless, indications of the rapidly growing urbanization in Pakistan are unmistakable. First, the share of the total urban population at the national and provincial levels, except in KP, has palpably increased over the past two and a half decades (Figure 5).[18] Second, the total national and provincial populations and their rural segments have grown at considerably lower rates than the urban population (Figure 6). Third, two megacities emerged

---

[16] Pakistan Bureau of Statistics. Population Census Final Results. Area and Population of Administrative Units (1998). Access may be requested.

[17] For example (i) the United Nations Development Programme (UNDP) in Pakistan in 2019 noted that while the government estimated the urban population at 36.44% of total population in 2017, other estimates "suggest that the ratio of urban to rural population could be 40% or even higher." See UNDP Pakistan. 2019. Sustainable Urbanization. *Development Advocate Pakistan*. 5 (4). p. 1; and (ii) even earlier on, using a geographic information system and an agglomeration index that combined travel time, population density, and biophysical and infrastructure variables as metrics, a study by the International Food Policy Research Institute (IFPRI) estimated that 70% of Pakistan's population in 2016 lived in peri-urban or urban areas. See: M. Kedir, E. Schmidt, and A. Waqas. 2016. Pakistan's Changing Demography: Urbanization and Peri-Urban Transformation Over Time. *Pakistan Strategy Support Program*. Working Paper. No. 39. IFPRI.

[18] Findings from the first nighttime light study conducted in Pakistan, which estimated district- and city-level economic activity in KP during 2005–2020, corroborate the provincial urban population growth pattern shown in Figure 5. Specifically, the study revealed a low and stagnating level of urbanization in KP in contrast to other provinces. See: S.M. Hasan, R.C.M. Beyer, and K. Hassan. 2021. *Policy Brief. GDP of Khyber Pakhtunkhwa's Districts. Measuring Economic Activity Using Nightlights*. The Government of Khyber Pakhtunkhwa, Sustainable Energy and Economic Development (program), Adam Smith International, and UK Aid Direct.

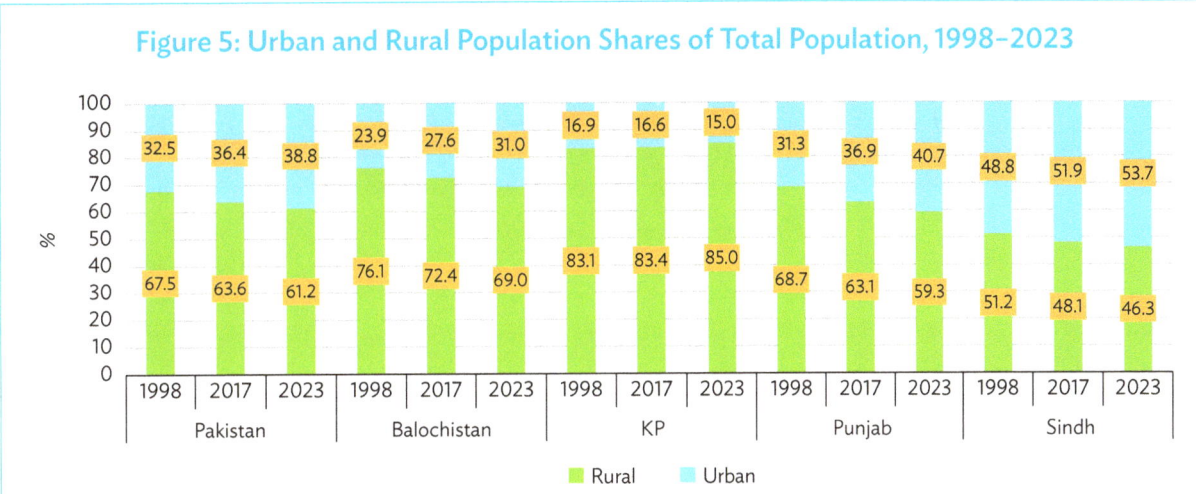

Figure 5: Urban and Rural Population Shares of Total Population, 1998–2023

KP = Khyber Pakhtunkhwa.

Notes:
1. The 1998 census covered 1981–1998; the 2017 census covered 1998–2017; and the 2023 digital census covered 2017–2023.
2. In the 1998 census, KP was still named North West Frontier Province.
3. The 2017 annual population growth rate of KP in Table 1 Final Results (Census–2023) includes that of the Federally Administered Tribal Areas, which were merged with KP in 2018. This explains the discrepancy in the 2017 population data of KP in the two reference tables.

Sources: Pakistan Bureau of Statistics. Table–1 Final Results (Census–2017); and Pakistan Bureau of Statistics. 2023. Announcement of Results of 7th Population and Housing Census–2023 'The Digital Census.' News release. 5 August.

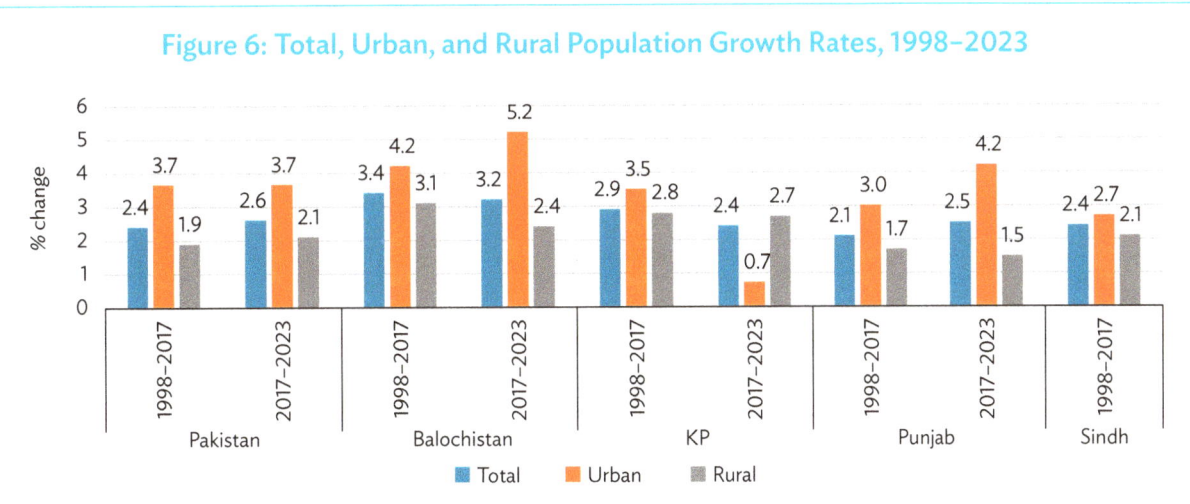

Figure 6: Total, Urban, and Rural Population Growth Rates, 1998–2023

KP = Khyber Pakhtunkhwa.

Notes:
1. The percentages reflect the average annual growth rates for the period.
2. In the 1998 census, KP was still named North West Frontier Province.
3. The 2017 annual population growth rate of KP in Table 1 Final Results (Census–2023) includes that of the Federally Administered Tribal Areas, which were merged with KP in 2018. This explains the discrepancy in the 2017 population data of KP in the two reference tables.

Source: Pakistan Bureau of Statistics. Table–1 Final Results (Census–2017) and Table 1 Final Results (Census–2023) 'The Digital Census'.

and are continually expanding—Karachi, with about 18 million people in 2023,[19] from 14.9 million people in 2017 (footnote 5); and Lahore, with 13 million people in 2023, up from 11.1 million in 2017. The urban populations in most districts and subdistricts in all provinces also rose at generally higher rates in 1998–2017 (footnote 7).

Meanwhile, even if Punjab continues to have the highest number of urban dwellers, at 52 million in 2023 (Figure 7), it comes second to Sindh in urbanization. Because of Karachi, Pakistan's largest city, Sindh has the highest urban population proportion, at 53.7% in 2023 (Figure 5), making it the country's most urbanized province, as it has been for several decades (footnote 16). The latest projections see the urban population climbing to 99.4 million or 40.7% of the country's total by 2030 and to 112.5 million or 43.1% of the total by 2035.[20] This will intensify the pressure on cities that continue to be mired in ever-increasing deficits in infrastructure and services.

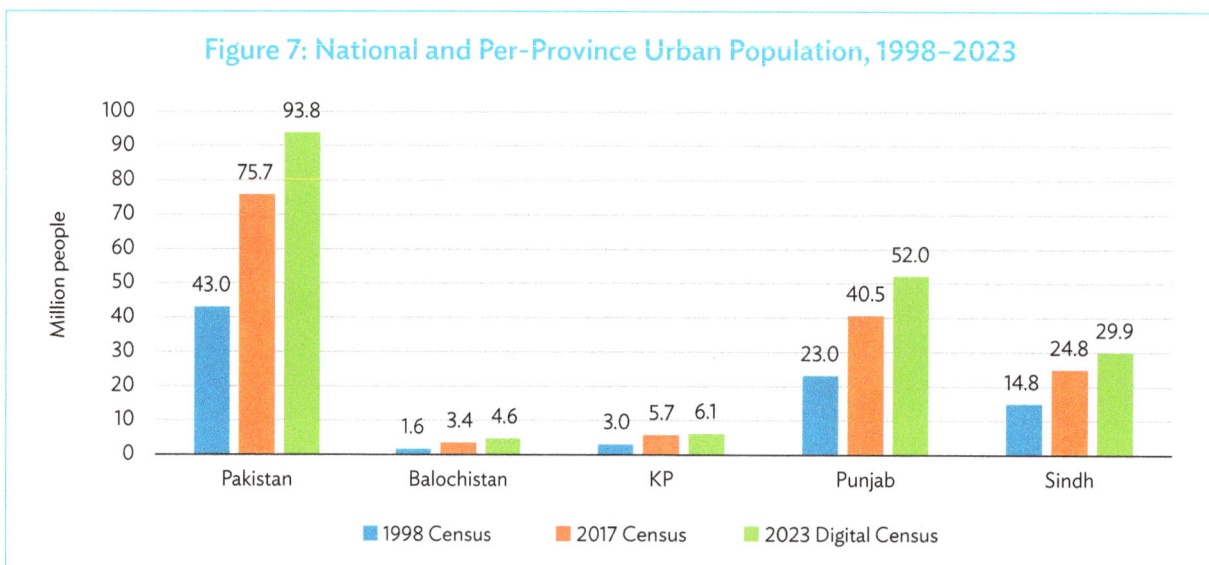

Figure 7: National and Per-Province Urban Population, 1998–2023

KP = Khyber Pakhtunkhwa.

Notes:
1. In the 1998 census, KP was still named North West Frontier Province.
2. The 2017 annual population growth rate of KP in Table 1 Final Results (Census–2023) includes that of the Federally Administered Tribal Areas, which were merged with KP in 2018. This explains the discrepancy in the 2017 population data of KP in the two reference documents.

Sources: Pakistan Bureau of Statistics. Table–1 Final Results (Census–2017); and Pakistan Bureau of Statistics. 2023. Announcement of Results of 7th Population and Housing Census–2023 'The Digital Census.' News release. 5 August.

Urban Centers Distribution

As Pakistan's urbanization has escalated, so has the trend toward the concentration of the urban population in a few urban centers. This is highlighted by the quick transformation of Karachi and Lahore into megacities. It is also evidenced by the 2017 census results showing 54.27% of the country's urban population living in just 21 urban localities with a population size of 500,000 and above (Table 2). Karachi and Lahore, both consisting of several

---

[19] Approximate figure reflecting the 4.1% annual increase reported by the 2023 digital census in the population of Karachi, the urban portion of which was estimated at 14.9 million by the 2017 census.
[20] United Nations Human Settlements Programme (UN-Habitat). 2022. *World Cities Report 2022. Envisaging the Future of Cities.*

urban localities,[21] comprised 34.5% of this population. In contrast, areas with fewer than 50,000 people, comprising 369 of the 588 designated urban localities in the 2017 census, accounted for only 12.44% of Pakistan's urban population. Meanwhile, of the 97 cities with 100,000 or more inhabitants, Punjab was home to 58, Sindh to 22, KP to 11, and Balochistan to 5. Islamabad stood as a single city.

Interestingly, while all 13 major cities of Pakistan saw their populations swell in 1972–1998, only three of them—Lahore, Peshawar, and Sialkot—experienced accelerating increases in 1998–2017 (Table 3). The slackening population growth in most big cities may indicate a shift in the direction of urbanization to smaller-sized, secondary, or intermediate cities and towns, within and across provinces. The shift, when supported by appropriate policies, strategies, and investments, can help decongest Pakistan's major cities and arrest the multifaceted deterioration many of them are facing. It can also trigger more balanced regional and urban development that bodes well for the growth of more sustainable and livable cities.

Table 2: Share of Urban Localities by Population Size in National Urban Population, 2017 Census

Population Size	Total Localities	Total Inhabitants	Share in National Urban Population (%)
500,000 and above	21	41,064,841	54.3
200,000 to 499,999	27	8,663,112	11.5
100,00 to 199,999	59	8,465,078	11.2
50,000 to 99,000	112	8,058,305	10.5
Below 50,000	369	9,419,501	12.4

Note: No corresponding data from the 2023 digital census have yet been published.
Source: Government of Pakistan, Ministry of Planning, Development and Special Initiatives. Pakistan Bureau of Statistics. Undated. *Pakistan National Census Report 2017*.

Table 3: Annual Population Change of Major Cities, 1972–2017

City (Province)	Population ('000)				Annual Change (%)		
	1972	1981	1998	2017	1972–1981	1981–1998	1998–2017
Karachi (Sindh)	3,515	5,208	9,339	14,884	0.6	4.7	3.1
Lahore (Punjab)	2,180	2,953	5,444	11,120	0.5	5.0	5.5
Faisalabad (Punjab)	823	1,104	2,009	3,210	0.4	4.8	3.2
Gujranwala (Punjab)	324	601	1,133	2,165	1.1	5.2	4.8
Rawalpindi (Punjab)	615	695	1,410	2,098	0.2	6.1	2.6
Peshawar (KP)	275	566	983	1,964	1.3	4.3	5.3
Multan (Punjab)	539	732	1,197	1,873	0.4	3.7	3.0

continued on next page

---

[21] An urban locality, in Pakistan's current usage, is different from a city, which is made up of one or more urban localities. As may be gleaned from *Pakistan National Census Report 2017*, urban localities are identified at census time following notification from provincial and/or local governments, including cantonment boards (footnote 5, p. 75).

Table 3 *continued*

City (Province)	Population ('000)				Annual Change (%)		
	1972	1981	1998	2017	1972–1981	1981–1998	1998–2017
Hyderabad (Sindh)	629	752	1,167	1,734	0.2	3.3	2.6
Islamabad (ICT)	77	204	529	1,009	2.1	9.4	4.8
Quetta (Balochistan)	158	286	760	999	1.0	9.8	1.7
Bahawalpur (Punjab)	134	180	408	763	0.4	7.4	4.6
Sargodha (Punjab)	200	291	458	658	0.6	3.4	2.3
Sialkot (Punjab)	204	302	422	657	0.6	2.3	3.0

ICT = Islamabad Capital Territory, KP = Khyber Pakhtunkhwa.

Notes: The 13 major cities included here are those with a population of 600,000 and above as of 2017. No corresponding data from the 2023 digital census have yet been published.

Source: Government of Pakistan, Ministry of Planning, Development and Special Initiatives. Pakistan Bureau of Statistics. Undated. *Pakistan National Census Report 2017.*

Rural–urban migration, within provinces and across provinces, contributed to the population growth of Pakistan's major cities. Nevertheless, except for eight cities and districts, official estimates place the incidence of both types of migration at below 10% of the total city and/or district population as of 2020 (Table 4).

Table 4: Migration Profile of Provinces and Major Cities or Districts, 2020
(% of population)

Province, City, or District		Native	Migrants	Intra-Provincial	Inter-Provincial
Balochistan	Province	96.5	3.5	2.1	1.5
	Quetta	88.3	11.7	6.5	5.2
KP	Province	95.7	4.4	3.9	0.4
	Peshawar	87.6	12.4	11.5	0.9
Punjab	Province	92.5	7.5	6.0	1.4
	Lahore	85.0	15.0	13.2	1.7
	Faisalabad	91.8	8.2	7.2	1.0
	Gujranwala	89.4	10.6	9.5	1.1
	Rawalpindi	85.0	15.0	7.4	7.7
	Bahawalpur	94.3	5.7	5.1	0.6
	Multan	94.8	5.2	4.5	0.7
	Sargodha	94.4	5.6	4.9	0.7
	Sialkot	93.2	6.8	6.0	0.9
Sindh	Province	94.4	5.6	3.3	2.4
	Karachi South	91.2	8.8	3.8	5.1
	Karachi Central	89.7	10.3	4.5	5.7
	Karachi West	88.5	11.4	2.6	8.8

continued on next page

Table 4 continued

Province, City, or District		Native	Migrants	Intra-Provincial	Inter-Provincial
	Karachi East	80.9	19.1	10.8	8.3
	Karachi Malir	93.9	6.1	4.8	1.3
	Korangi	95.4	4.6	2.3	2.3
	Islamabad	64.0	36.0	17.0	19.0

ICT = Islamabad Capital Territory, KP = Khyber Pakhtunkhwa.
Notes:
1. Figures may not add up because of rounding.
2. Figures for Islamabad are rounded off in the source document.

Source: Pakistan Bureau of Statistics. *Pakistan Social and Living Standards Measurement Survey (2019–20) National/Provincial/District*. Table 6.

Until 2017, Pakistan's urban centers remained concentrated in Punjab and Sindh (Figure 8). Many of the cities across the provinces are confronting mounting challenges from unplanned and unmanaged urbanization. A growing number have sprawled into open areas and along roads, rail tracks, *nullahs* (ravines), and other public lands at the heart of cities or outlying localities.

The Global Urban Footprint, produced by German scientists using radar technology, has shown Pakistan's urban footprint to vary among the provinces (Figure 9). As of 2016, urban settlements were generally scattered across Punjab, except the arid southeastern part of the province. They were proximate to the capital cities of Quetta in Balochistan and Peshawar in KP, and overconcentrated in Karachi in Sindh. Data from the Pakistan Demographic Survey 2020 (footnote 12) and the 2023 digital census (footnote 2) suggest no essential shift in these urban expansion patterns until recently.

Most of Pakistan's cities are in the Indus River's fertile lands and the Punjab plains. The continuing unmanaged expansion of these cities has thus meant unconstrained urban encroachments into agricultural lands (Figure 10). The extent and progress of these encroachments, which put the country's future food security at risk, need to be monitored and accounted for in urban policy development at the provincial and federal levels.

Pakistan's urban footprint map reveals an emerging continuous linear urban area that forms an arc shape connecting Lahore to Peshawar (Figure 11). This linear urban development, also observable in various parts of Punjab, particularly between Lahore and Faisalabad and Lahore and Multan, follows the ecumenopolis concept introduced by Constantinos Apostolou Doxiadis in the 1960s. This is a thought experiment surrounding the idea that in the future, urban areas will eventually fuse into a planetwide city. While highly unlikely, the idea may be a useful catalyst for discussions about the future of urbanization, the environment, and technology.

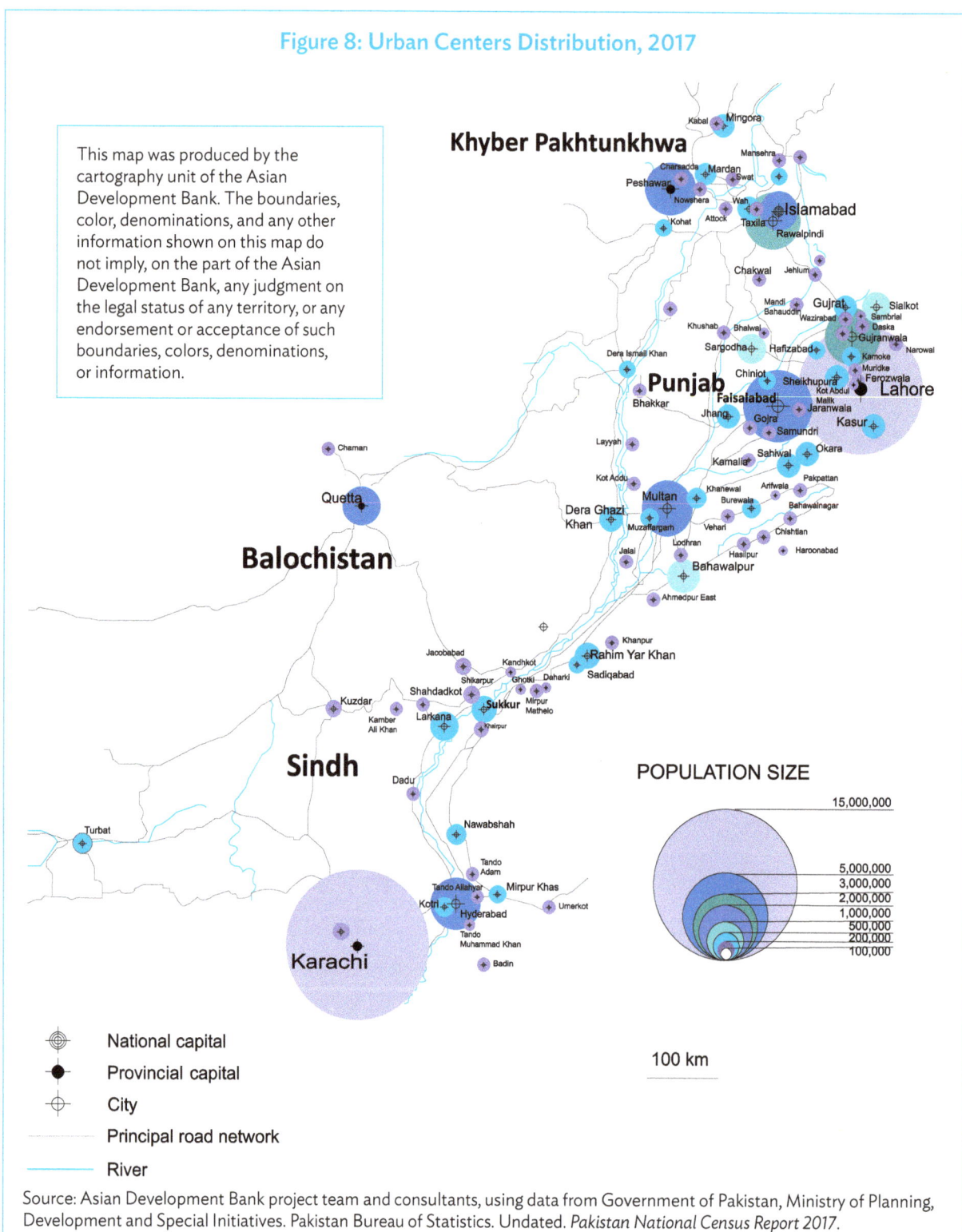

Figure 8: Urban Centers Distribution, 2017

Source: Asian Development Bank project team and consultants, using data from Government of Pakistan, Ministry of Planning, Development and Special Initiatives. Pakistan Bureau of Statistics. Undated. *Pakistan National Census Report 2017*.

Figure 9: Urban Footprint, 2016

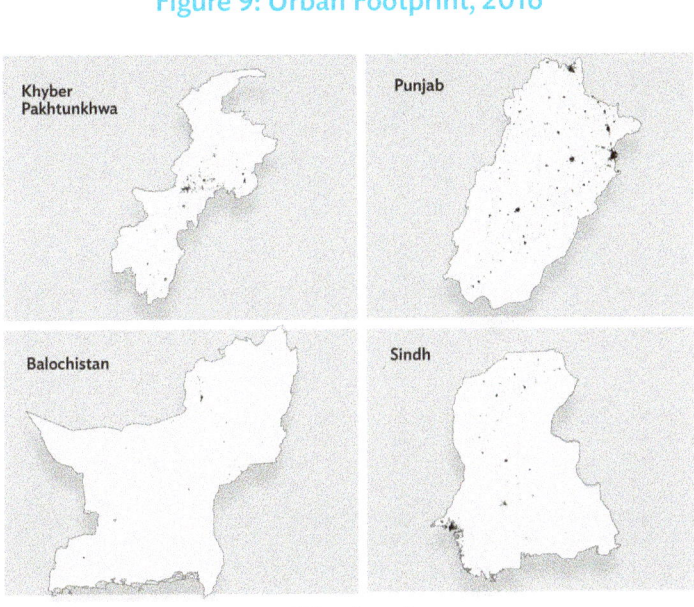

• Urban footprint

Source: Project consultants, using data from German Aerospace Center, Earth Observation Center (accessed 8 October 2021). These data are now available at: European Union. European Data. Global Urban Footprint (GUF) - TSX/TDX – Global.

Figure 10: Urban Encroachments into Agricultural Lands, 2017

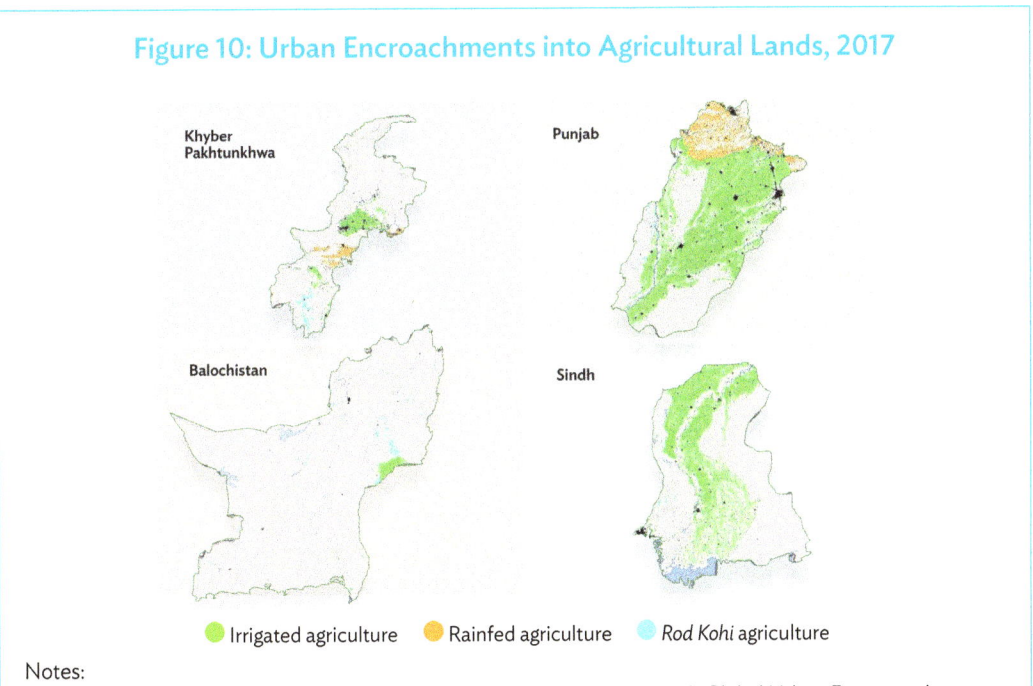

● Irrigated agriculture   ● Rainfed agriculture   ● *Rod Kohi* agriculture

Notes:
Maps were derived from the juxtaposition of Pakistan's *Land Use Atlas* with Global Urban Footprint data. *Rod Kohi* is an upland rainwater harvesting irrigation system in Pakistan.

Source: Project consultants, using data from Government of Pakistan, Ministry of Environment. 2009. *Land Use Atlas* (for background map); and German Aerospace Center, Earth Observation Center (for urban footprint map). The urban footprint data are now available at: European Union. European Data. Global Urban Footprint (GUF) - TSX/TDX - Global.

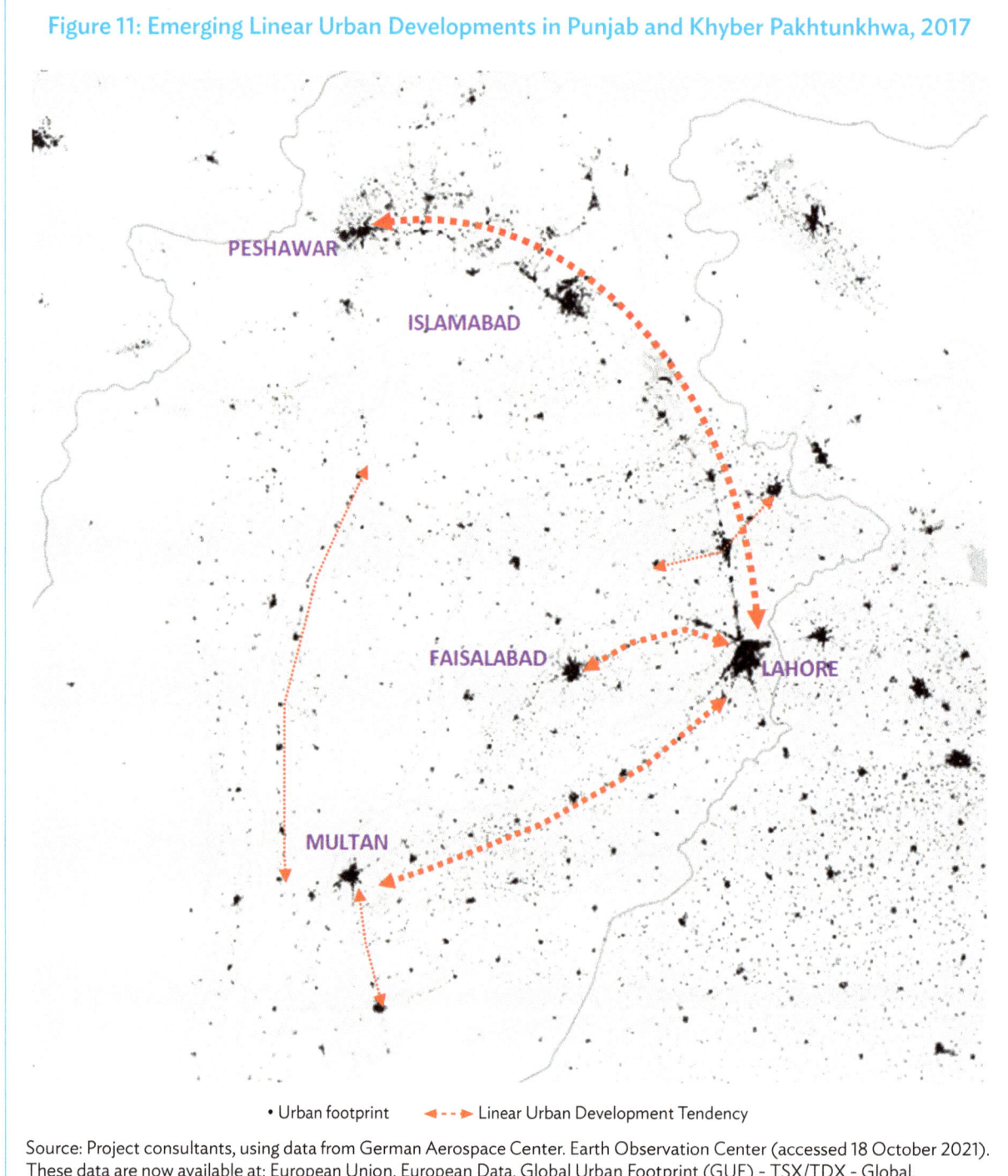

Figure 11: Emerging Linear Urban Developments in Punjab and Khyber Pakhtunkhwa, 2017

• Urban footprint   ◄--► Linear Urban Development Tendency

Source: Project consultants, using data from German Aerospace Center. Earth Observation Center (accessed 18 October 2021). These data are now available at: European Union. European Data. Global Urban Footprint (GUF) - TSX/TDX - Global.

Economic Environment

Economic Performance

Rapid urbanization is occurring unabated amid an uncertain macroeconomic environment in Pakistan. While the country had the world's fifth-largest population in 2021,[22] its economy ranked only 42nd globally in nominal gross domestic product (GDP)[23] and 173rd in per capita GDP.[24] Low economic productivity—rooted in stagnating labor productivity, lack of domestic savings and investment, and a narrow production base—has worsened with economic misalignment, increasing resource constraints, and unprecedented disasters in the last few years.

Particularly, economic policies that fuel consumption and short-term growth but disregard their structural impacts have brought about cycles of boom and bust featuring severe internal and external imbalances. The latest of these cycles saw GDP decline sharply even before the coronavirus disease (COVID-19) outbreak, plunging to 0.94% negative growth in fiscal year (FY) 2020 mainly because of the pandemic (Figure 12).

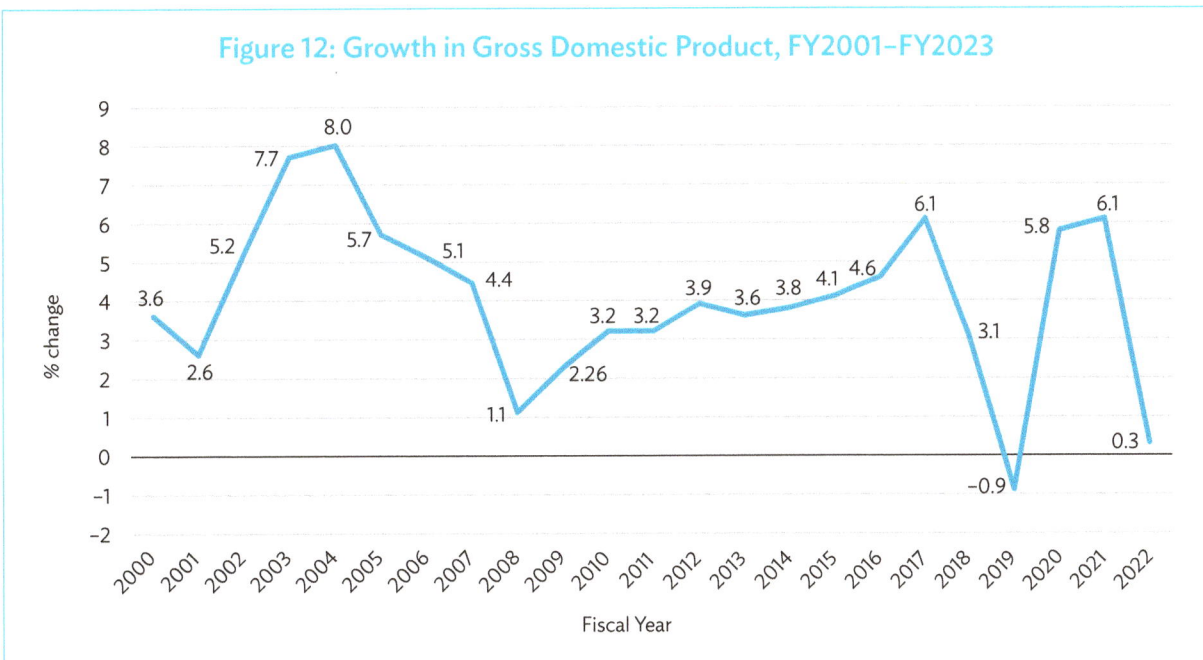

FY = fiscal year.

Notes:
1. The fiscal year of the Government of Pakistan ends on 30 June. "FY" before a calendar year denotes the year in which the fiscal year ends, e.g., FY2023 ends on 30 June 2023.
2. Gross domestic product figures for 2000 to 2016 are based on FY2006 constant prices, and from 2017 onward are based on FY2016 constant prices.

Source: Pakistan Bureau of Statistics. National Accounts Tables. Table 01. Macroeconomic Indicators (accessed 16 November 2023).

---

[22] State Bank of Pakistan. 2022. *Annual Report 2021–2022. The State of Pakistan's Economy*.
[23] World Development Indicators. Gross Domestic Product 2022 (accessed 10 May 2023).
[24] World Population Review (accessed 23 March 2023).

In response, the government backpedaled from its 2019 market-driven exchange rate policy and fiscal consolidation agenda to increase money supply and domestic demand. Lower interest rates and a host of fiscal stimulus measures, including higher-than-budgeted fuel and electricity subsidies, elevated public wages and pensions, tax exemptions, and a real estate tax amnesty, enabled GDP to recover and grow by 5.77% in FY2021 and 6.10% in FY2022.[25]

However, macroeconomic vulnerabilities quickly sprang up as import costs significantly outstripped export earnings on the back of increased domestic demand and a steep rise in global oil and commodity prices.[26] Fiscal slippages, limited cash inflows, and sluggish structural reforms aggravated macroeconomic deterioration. Inflation rose to double-digit levels due to the sizable depreciation of the Pakistan rupee, upward fuel and electricity adjustments, and global inflationary pressures from geopolitical tensions. By the end of FY2022, Pakistan's current account and fiscal deficits bulged despite the curtailment of some expansionary macroeconomic policies and improved tax revenues.

With additional constraints from dwindling international reserves, tight foreign exchange control, massive flood damages and economic losses, and political instability, GDP growth plunged to 0.29% in FY2023, and headline inflation largely reflecting high food prices, averaged 29.2%, the country's highest in the last 5 decades to 2023.[27] While downside risks will remain significant, including from global price shocks and slower global growth, GDP growth is projected to recover modestly to 1.9% in FY2024, and inflation will ease to 25%. But these near-term prospects will rely heavily on the progress of an economic adjustment program supported by international development partners. The adjustment program aims to stabilize the economy and rebuild fiscal and external buffers. It involves fiscal consolidation, a market-determined exchange rate, reforms in the energy sector and state-owned enterprises, expanded social and development spending, and related governance and institutional reforms.

Sector Analysis

In contrast to their remarkable performance in FY2021 and FY2022, all major sectors slowed down in FY2023 (Figure 13). Agricultural output grew by only 1.6%, compared to 4.4% the previous year, its highest growth rate since FY2017. Services output rose by only 0.9% compared to 6.6% in FY2022, also its peak growth rate since FY2017. Industrial production declined to negative 0.9%, against 6.8% growth in FY2022.

Notwithstanding the sharp fluctuations in sectoral growth, the sector shares in GDP varied only slightly in the last 5 years (Figure 14), a trend that goes back to over a decade ago (footnote 28) and suggests a negligible shift in recent times in the sectoral structure of the economy.

---

[25] Government of Pakistan. Pakistan Bureau of Statistics. National Accounts Tables. Table 1. Macroeconomic Indicators (accessed 10 October 2023).
[26] ADB. Pakistan Resident Mission. 2023. Country Information Notes. March (available on request).
[27] ADB. 2023. *Asian Development Outlook September 2023*.

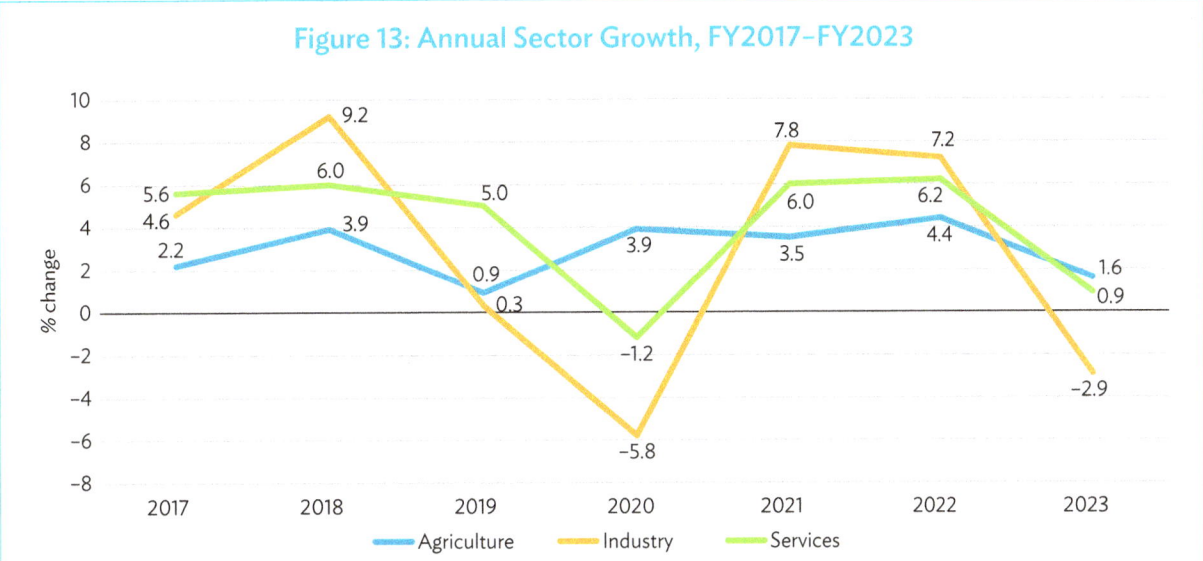

Figure 13: Annual Sector Growth, FY2017–FY2023

FY = fiscal year.

Notes:
1. Data for FY2021 to FY2023 are provisional.
2. The fiscal year of the Government of Pakistan ends on 30 June. "FY" before a calendar year denotes the year in which the fiscal year ends, e.g., FY2023 ends on 30 June 2023.

Sources: Government of Pakistan, Finance Division. *Pakistan Economic Survey 2021–22*. Table 1.3 Growth Rates (2017–2022 data), and Asian Development Bank. 2023. *Asian Development Outlook September 2023* (2023 data).

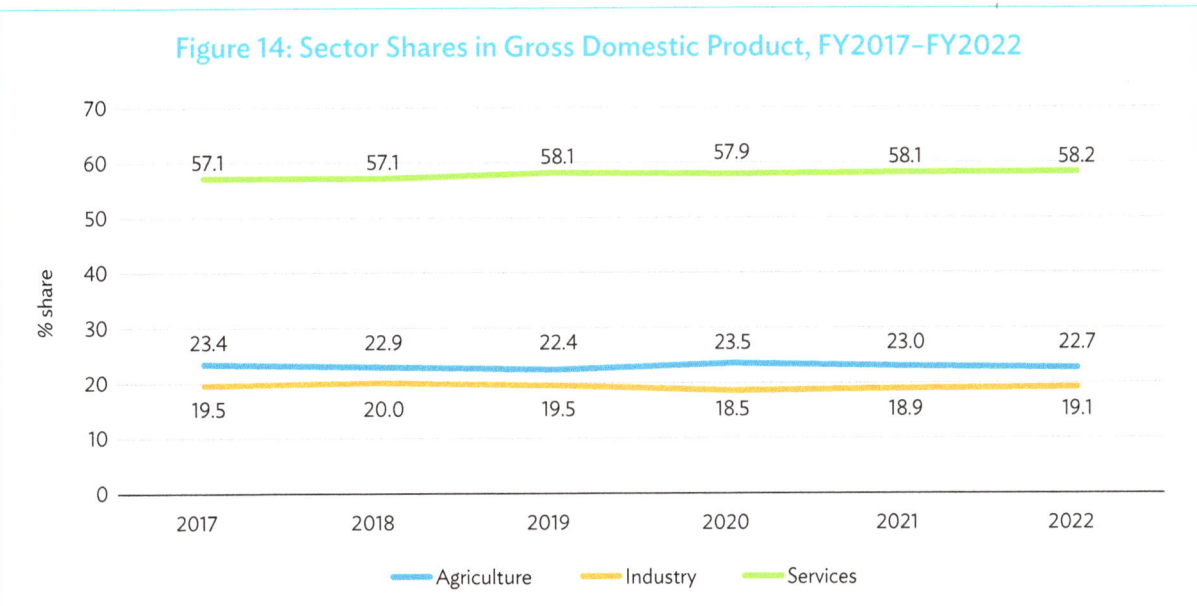

Figure 14: Sector Shares in Gross Domestic Product, FY2017–FY2022

FY = fiscal year.

Notes:
1. Data for FY2023 is not yet available.
2. The fiscal year of the Government of Pakistan ends on 30 June. "FY" before a calendar year denotes the year in which the fiscal year ends, e.g., FY2023 ends on 30 June 2023.

Source: Government of Pakistan. Finance Division. *Pakistan Economic Survey 2021–22*. Table 1.2. Sectoral Share in GDP (%).

The Finance Department of Punjab, however, reported in its latest budget strategy paper that Pakistan's GDP structure changed significantly between 1950 and 2021.[28] Agriculture's share declined by 30.0%, services rose by 21.2%, and manufacturing by 8.9% of GDP (Figure 15).

However, while the services sector provided comparatively less employment, the increase in jobs in the manufacturing sector also indicated only a gradual migration from agriculture (Figure 16). This reflects Pakistan's lack of focus on growth in business or manufacturing, which the Punjab budget strategy paper argues is "one of the major factors contributing to premature de-industrialization and a skewed structural transformation in favour of the services sector."

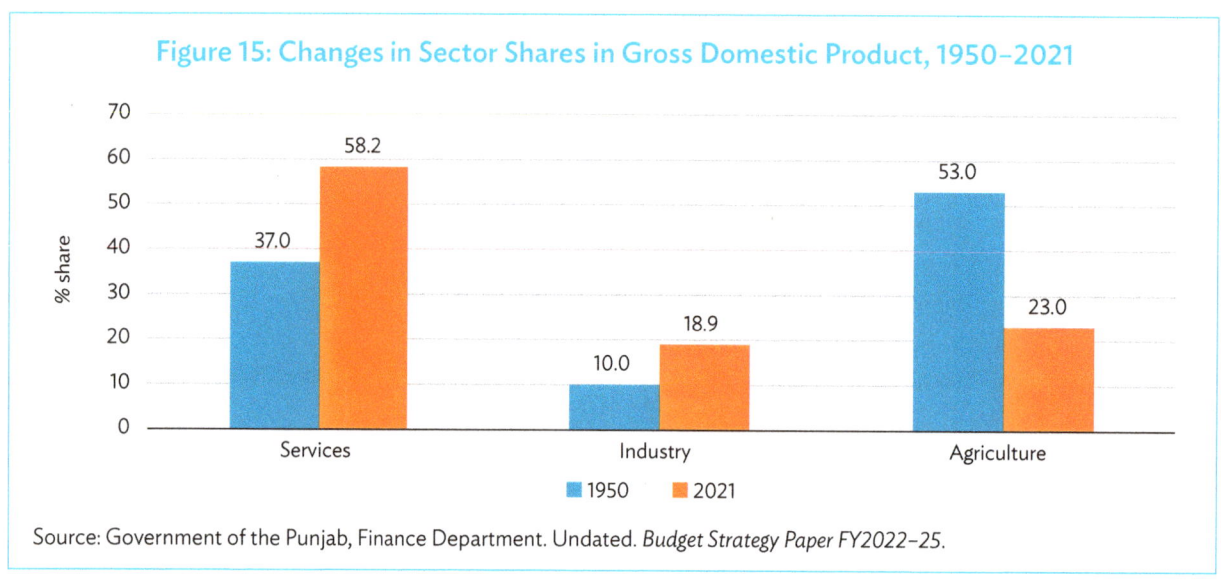

Source: Government of the Punjab, Finance Department. Undated. *Budget Strategy Paper FY2022–25*.

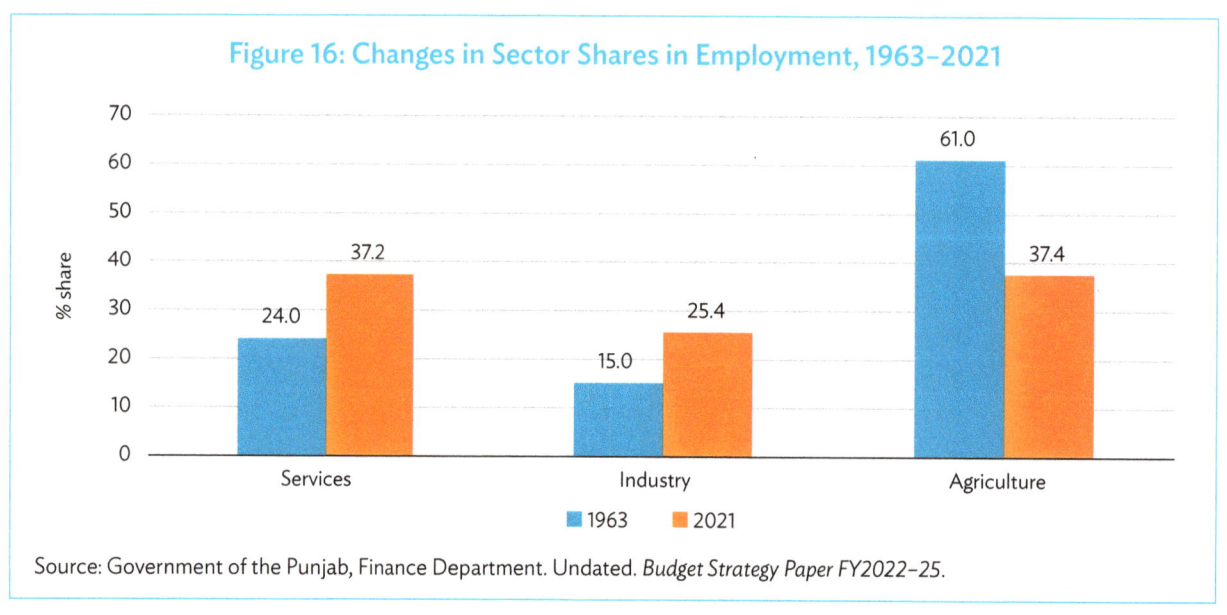

Source: Government of the Punjab, Finance Department. Undated. *Budget Strategy Paper FY2022–25*.

---

[28] Government of the Punjab. Finance Department. *Budget Strategy Paper FY2022–25*.

The excessive supply of agricultural labor and lack of job creation have facilitated the growth of a large informal sector, which significantly contributes to Pakistan's economy but is fraught with social issues and creates vulnerabilities for formal businesses. In FY2021, the informal sector accounted for 72.5% of employment nationwide, 76.2% in rural areas, and 68.5% in urban areas.[29] It averaged 33% of GDP from 2000 to 2018.[30]

Other Lingering Constraints

Highlighting how recent experiences brought to the fore the need to address structural economic weaknesses, the State Bank of Pakistan's 2022 annual report (footnote 22) provides more information on how these weaknesses played out amid the country's upbeat economic performance in FY2021–FY2022. Investment lagged, rising by just 0.3% of GDP between FY2020 and FY2022. Wage increases occurred in most sectors but at levels below the inflation rate. Unemployment slightly dropped from 6.9% in FY2019 to 6.3% in FY2021 but showed a reversal in prospects toward the end of FY2022. Moreover, despite hitting for the first time the $30 billion mark in absolute value in FY2022, the country's exports continued to grow much less and slower than imports (Table 5). All these lingering constraints amplified the economic impacts of the severe shocks that battered Pakistan in FY2023.[31]

Table 5: Merchandise Exports and Imports, FY2017–FY2022

Item	FY2017	FY2018	FY2019	FY2020	FY2021	FY2022
Export growth rate, %	0.1	12.6	(2.1)	(7.1)	13.8	26.6
Import growth rate, %	16.4	16.0	(6.8)	(15.9)	24.4	32.8
Export value, % of GDP	6.5	6.9	7.5	7.5	7.4	8.6
Import value, % of GDP	(14.1)	(15.6)	(16.1)	(14.5)	(15.6)	(19.2)
Trade balance, % of GDP	(7.7)	(8.7)	(8.6)	(7.0)	(8.2)	(10.5)

( ) = negative, ADB = Asian Development Bank, FY = fiscal year, GDP = gross domestic product.

Notes:
1. The fiscal year of the Government of Pakistan ends on 30 June. "FY" before a calendar year denotes the year in which the fiscal year ends, e.g., FY2023 ends on 30 June 2023.
2. Pakistan also exports and imports services, which is not reflected here because of lack of data.

Source: ADB. Pakistan Resident Mission. Country Information Notes. March 2023 (available on request).

The State Bank's 2022 annual report also attributed Pakistan's chronic trade deficit to its low value-added, low-priced commodity exports and a reliance on costly imports for industrial raw materials and machinery requirements (Table 6).[32] Breaking out of this unsustainable paradigm, the report added, will require transforming industry to a technology-intensive sector with the capacity to produce more sophisticated, in-demand goods and

---

[29] Government of Pakistan, Ministry of Planning, Development and Special Initiatives. Pakistan Bureau of Statistics. 2022. *Pakistan Labour Force Survey 2020-21*. The publication also defines the informal sector as comprising industrial units not registered under the Factories Act 1934, with less than 10 employees all without regular employee status.
[30] F. Ohnsorge and S. Yu, eds. 2022. *The Long Shadow of Informality. Challenges and Policies*. World Bank Group.
[31] Among others (i) industrial employment in Punjab and Sindh declined notably following a significant contraction in large-scale manufacturing output (e.g.,textile, food, pharmaceuticals, petroleum refining, automobiles); (ii) investment fell to 13.6% of GDP from 15.7% in FY2022 and 14.5% in FY2021; and (iii) exports shrunk by 14.1% and imports by 27.3% in FY2023. See: State Bank of Pakistan. 2023. *Annual Report 2022-2023. The State of Pakistan's Economy*.
[32] A detailed review of this chronic trade deficit is also in K. Rosbach and L. Aleksanyan. 2019. Why Pakistan's Economic Growth Continues to be Balance-of-Payments Constrained. *ADB Central and West Asia Working Paper Series*. No. 8. ADB.

services for export. This would necessitate an enabling policy framework and enormous investment in physical and human resource development.

Table 6: Major Exports and Imports, FY2021 and FY2022

Principal Exports, FY2021	% of Total	Principal Imports, FY2021	% of Total
Textiles and textile articles	56.5	Mineral products	21.1
Vegetable products	12.8	Machinery and mechanical appliances	15.1
Mineral products	4.3	Chemical products	11.1
Animal products	3.3	Textiles and textile articles	8.9
Food products	3.1	Base metals	8.5
Major Export Destinations, FY2022	% of Total	Major Import Sources, FY2022	% of Total
United States	21.2	People's Republic of China	26.2
People's Republic of China	10.0	United Arab Emirates	11.1
United Kingdom	6.8	Kingdom of Saudi Arabia	6.5
Germany	5.5	Indonesia	5.8
Netherlands	5.5	United States	5.0

ADB = Asian Development Bank, FY = fiscal year.
Notes:
1. The fiscal year of the Government of Pakistan ends on 30 June. "FY" before a calendar year denotes the year in which the fiscal year ends, e.g., FY2023 ends on 30 June 2023.
2. Pakistan export and import of services are not included here because of lack of data.

Source: ADB. Pakistan Resident Mission. Country Information Notes. March 2023 (available on request).

Meanwhile, remittances, which have historically cushioned Pakistan from its constant trade deficit, dropped by 13.6% to $27 billion in FY2023 (footnote 31) after continuously increasing and aggregating $105.6 billion between FY2019 and FY2022 (footnote 22). Besides the global economic slowdown, the resumption of cross-border air travel and the marked difference between interbank and open market rates accounted for the sharp decline (footnote 31).

Enabling Environment for Urban Competitiveness

Several global benchmarking initiatives, weighing in to support policy development and investment decisions, have offered insights on Pakistan's business environment and urban and economic competitiveness.

The World Economic Forum's Global Competitiveness Index 2019 gave Pakistan its best marks in market size and business dynamism, although it ranked the country three places lower than the previous year to 110th of 141 economies.[33] Pakistan fared worst in information and communication technology adoption, including fixed broadband and fiber internet, but had a competitive edge in shareholder governance, the prominence of research institutions, venture capital availability, and flexibility in hiring and firing workers. Its competitive disadvantages were terrorism incidence, applied trade tariffs, the ratio of female to male workers, and public debt prospects.

---

[33] K. Schwab, ed. 2019. *Insight Report. The Global Competitiveness Report 2019.* World Economic Forum.

In 2020, the World Bank identified Pakistan as one of the top 10 countries with the most notable improvement in ease of doing business, ranking it 108th of 190 economies.[34] The bank specifically cited Pakistan's success in improving procedures to start a business, obtain construction permits, get electricity, register property, pay taxes, and trade across borders.

Spatial Distribution of Economic Activities

Economic activities across the provinces of Pakistan are broadly similar. As with the national economy, agriculture remains dominant, but industries are thriving, and the services sector is catching up fast. Notwithstanding the broad similarities, wide disparities have persisted in the level of development and performance of the provincial economies (Table 7).

Table 7: Provincial Economic Output, FY2014–FY2020

Indicators	FY2014	FY2015	FY2016	FY2017	FY2018	FY2019	FY2020
Balochistan							
Provincial GDP ($ billion)	5.50	5.53	5.51	5.84	5.73	4.92	4.23
Share in National GDP (%)	5.31	5.27	5.17	5.23	5.10	5.32	5.33
GDP per capita ($)	492	480	462	474	…	…	323
KP							
Provincial GDP ($ billion)	10.78	9.09	9.29	10.15	10.76	9.19	8.25
Share in national GDP (%)	10.42	9.13	8.71	9.09	9.57	9.93	10.39
GDP per capita ($)	395	316	314	332	…	…	224
Punjab							
Provincial GDP ($ billion)	58.54	57.10	60.12	65.33	66.70	55.48	48.08
Share in national GDP (%)	56.58	54.41	56.37	58.47	59.36	59.92	62.58
GDP per capita ($)	572	546	563	599	…	…	406
Sindh							
Provincial GDP ($ billion)	28.65	32.74	31.72	30.41	29.19	23.00	18.81
Share in national GDP (%)	27.69	31.19	29.75	27.22	25.98	24.84	23.70
GDP per capita ($)	643	717	679	635	…	…	361

… = no data available, FY = fiscal year, GDP = gross domestic product, KP = Khyber Pakhtunkhwa.

Notes:
1. Provincial GDP figures and their corresponding shares in the national GDP reflect the estimates generated by the pioneering nighttime lights study undertaken by the Government of KP and development partners.
2. The GDP estimates, calculated by the study by distributing the national GDP in proportion to each province's share in nighttime lights (for nonagricultural activity) and rural population (for agricultural activity), were originally in Pakistan rupees. They were converted to dollars using archived exchange rate figures from the State Bank of Pakistan.
3. Estimates of the GDP per capita were based on population figures released by the Pakistan Bureau of Statistics.
4. The fiscal year of the Government of Pakistan ends on 30 June. "FY" before a calendar year denotes the year in which the fiscal year ends, e.g., FY2023 ends on 30 June 2023.

Source: Asian Development Bank project team estimates, using data from (i) S.M. Hasan, R.C.M. Beyer, and K. Hassan. 2021. *Policy Brief. GDP of Khyber Pakhtunkhwa's Districts. Measuring Economic Activity Using Nightlights*. The Government of Khyber Pakhtunkhwa, Sustainable Energy and Economic Development (program), Adam Smith International, and UK Aid Direct; (ii) State Bank of Pakistan. Core Statistics Department. Historical Exchange Rates. Monthly Average Exchange Rates; and (iii) Pakistan Bureau of Statistics. Table-1 Final Results (Census-2017) and *Pakistan Demographic Survey-2020*.

---

[34] World Bank. Data. Ease of Doing Business in Pakistan (accessed 8 November 2021).

The provincial GDP findings revealed a strong correlation between urban development and economic growth and prosperity. For instance, Punjab, with eight of the 13 major cities identified in the 2017 census report (Table 3), also comprises Pakistan's biggest provincial economy. However, it is also evident in Punjab that a larger economy or higher economic output does not always mean greater income per capita, with the province second to Sindh in GDP per capita, at least before the COVID-19 pandemic.

Employment

Reflecting the provincial mix of economic activities, agriculture generated the most employment in Balochistan and Punjab in 2021, while the services sector did so in KP and Sindh (Figure 17).

However, in Pakistan's major cities, services and industry were the main employment sectors (Figure 18). With the same employment pattern in 2018, the cities generated 55% of the country's GDP. Ten major cities contributed 95% of federal tax revenue. Karachi alone accounted for 12%–15% of national GDP and 55% of federal tax revenue.[35]

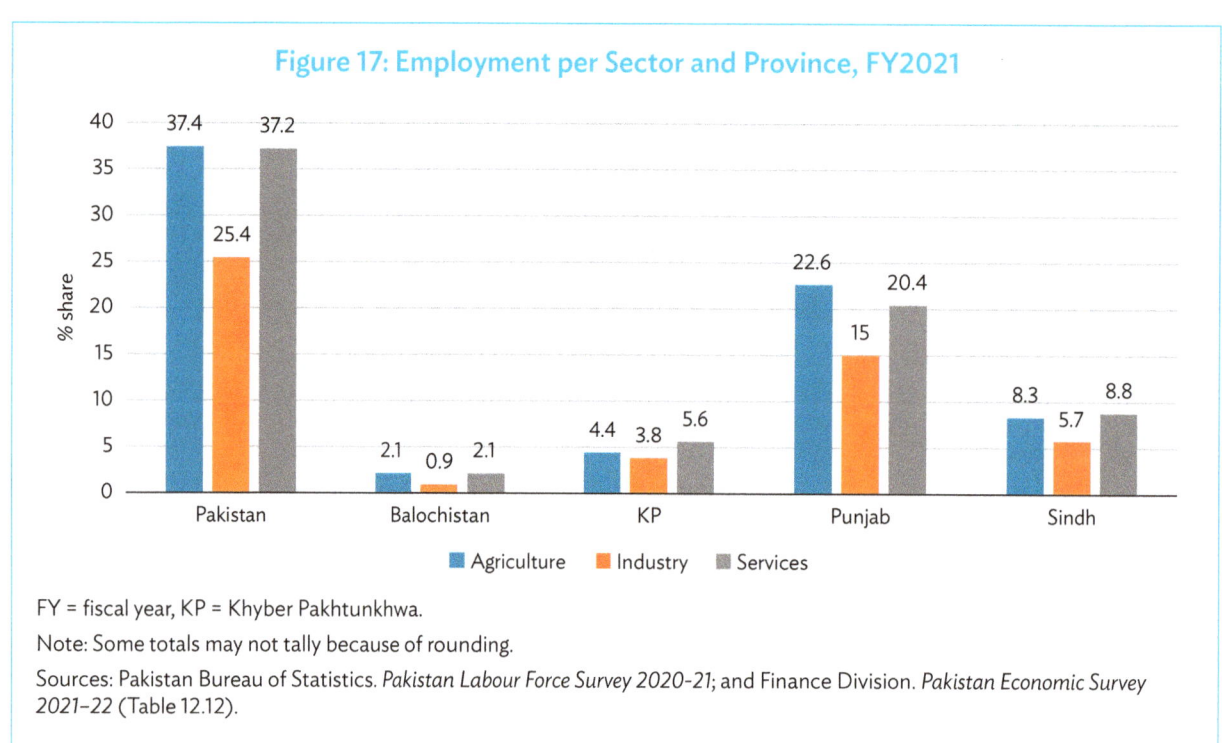

Figure 17: Employment per Sector and Province, FY2021

FY = fiscal year, KP = Khyber Pakhtunkhwa.
Note: Some totals may not tally because of rounding.
Sources: Pakistan Bureau of Statistics. *Pakistan Labour Force Survey 2020-21*; and Finance Division. *Pakistan Economic Survey 2021–22* (Table 12.12).

---

[35] UN-Habitat; Government of Pakistan, Ministry of Climate Change; and Australian Aid. 2018. *The State of Pakistani Cities 2018*. UN-Habitat.

Figure 18: Employment per Sector in Major Cities, FY2021

FY = fiscal year.
Note: From left to right, the cities are arranged from biggest to smallest in terms of population size.
Source: Pakistan Bureau of Statistics. *Pakistan Labour Force Survey 2020–21*.

Social Equity Profile

Latest Trends

Since 2021, Pakistan has endured multiple shocks, setting back poverty reduction and social development gains in the last 2 decades. As of October 2023, the World Bank estimated poverty could go up by 5.2% in just a year, from 34.2% in 2022 to 39.4% in 2023.[36] Considering population growth, this would translate into 12.5 million more Pakistanis living below the poverty line. But even before that, nonmonetary poverty indicators had already deteriorated. Mainly due to damages caused by floods on key infrastructure in water and sanitation, health, and education, more than 2.6 million enrolled children suffered significant learning losses, health care services became inaccessible to one-third of the population in worst-affected districts, and disrupted access to safe drinking water and sanitation magnified the risk of stunting and malnutrition.

Past Gains and Gaps

National-level poverty reduction. Aggregate poverty incidence in Pakistan, currently officially measured in terms of the cost of basic needs, sharply declined from 50.4% in 2005 to 21.9% in 2019 (Figure 19). This translated to an enormous reduction in poverty head count from 88 million to 48 million during the period. Studies attribute the sharp decline to multiple factors, primarily the expansion of male off-farm economic opportunities in the informal sector and increase in out-migration and associated remittances.[37]

---

[36] M. Meyer. 2023. *Poverty & Equity Brief. South Asia. Pakistan*. October. World Bank Group.
[37] World Bank. South Asia. 2020. *Islamic Republic of Pakistan. Leveling the Playing Field. Systematic Country Diagnostic*.

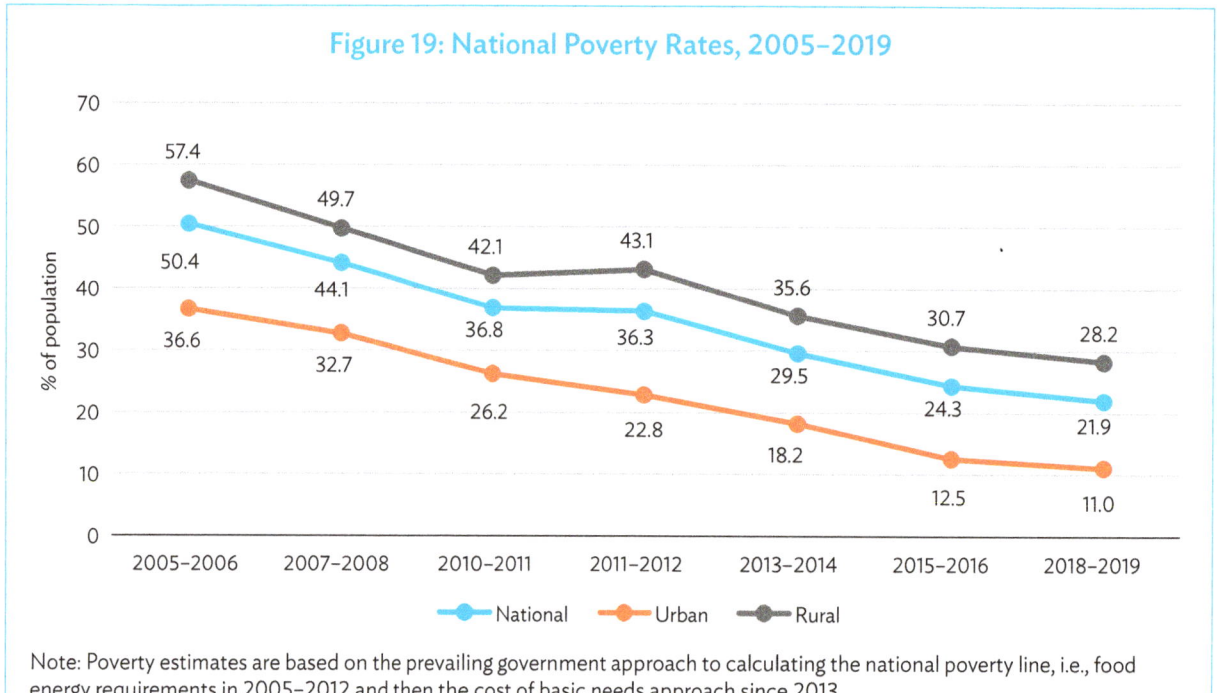

Figure 19: National Poverty Rates, 2005–2019

Note: Poverty estimates are based on the prevailing government approach to calculating the national poverty line, i.e., food energy requirements in 2005–2012 and then the cost of basic needs approach since 2013.
Source: Government of Pakistan, Finance Division. *Pakistan Economic Survey 2021-22*.

However, it is important to note that despite registering bigger declines through most of 2005 to 2019, rural poverty remained much more widespread than urban poverty. Rural poverty incidence was more than double that of urban poverty from 2015 to 2019. The staggering disparity reflected in the 81% share of the rural population in the latest national poverty statistics, could spark more rural–urban migration and worsen urbanization challenges. Careful consideration of the complex dynamics in rural–urban interactions and the incorporation of solutions to potential problems in both urban and rural development strategies will help mitigate development risks on both sides of the urban–rural nexus.

Poverty reduction across the provinces. In all provinces, poverty incidence declined significantly with urban and rural poverty registering double-digit decreases between 2005 and 2019 (Figure 20). Despite this, poverty head count ratios remained high and rural–urban disparity was significant. As of 2019, rural poverty stood at 47% in Balochistan, 29% in KP, 21% in Punjab, and 40% in Sindh. Urban poverty was at 25% in Balochistan, 17% in KP, 9% in Punjab, and 10% in Sindh, bringing the total of Pakistan's urban poor to around 8.5 million in 2019—3.9 million in Punjab, 2.6 million in Sindh, and 1.0 million each in Balochistan and KP.

Multidimensional poverty. Baseline data on multidimensional poverty generated by Pakistan's Planning Commission, the United Nations Development Programme (UNDP), and the Oxford Poverty and Human Development Initiatives (OPHI) in 2016 confirmed the continuous decline in poverty from 2004 to 2015. However, they showcased an even greater disparity between rural and urban poverty (Figure 21).[38] They also bared important differences among the provinces, with the multidimensional poverty index (MPI) reflecting the existing gaps in the ability of municipalities to offer the opportunities provided by cities in health, education, and better quality of life.

---

[38] Government of Pakistan, Ministry of Planning, Development and Reform. Planning Commission. 2016. *Multidimensional Poverty in Pakistan*. UNDP.

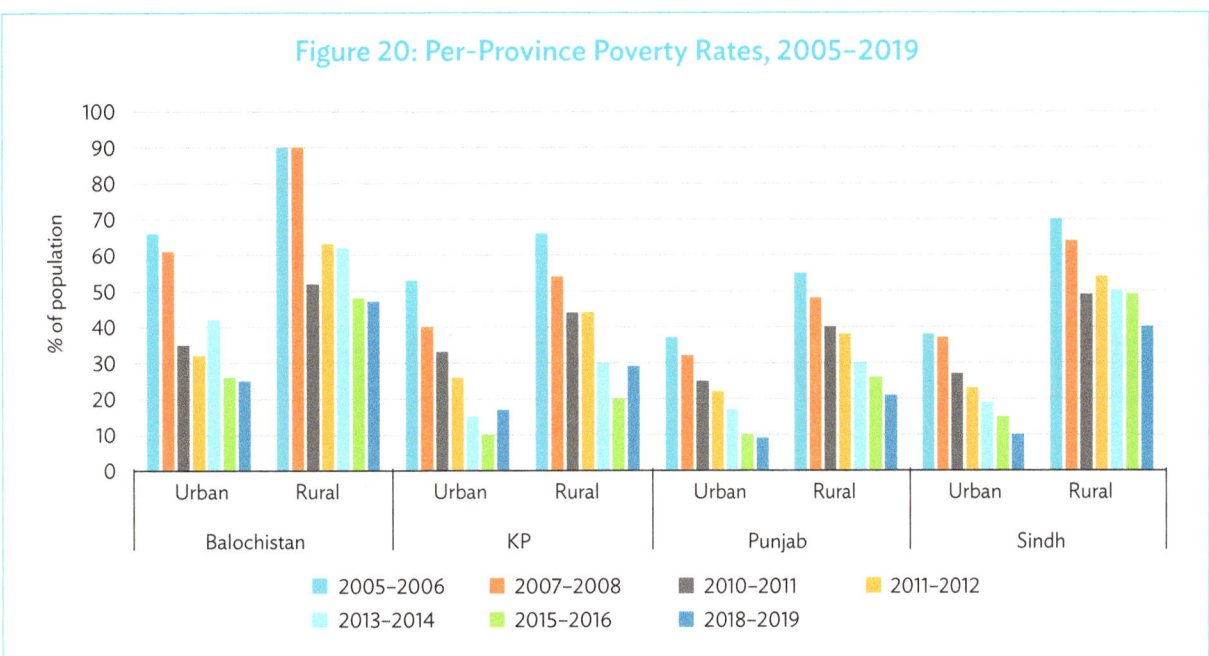

Figure 20: Per-Province Poverty Rates, 2005–2019

KP = Khyber Pakhtunkhwa.
Note: Poverty estimates are based on the prevailing government approach to calculating the national poverty line, i.e., food energy requirements in 2005–2012 and then the cost of basic needs approach since 2013.
Source: Pakistan Institute of Development Economics (PIDE). 2021. *The State of Poverty in Pakistan. PIDE Report 2021.*

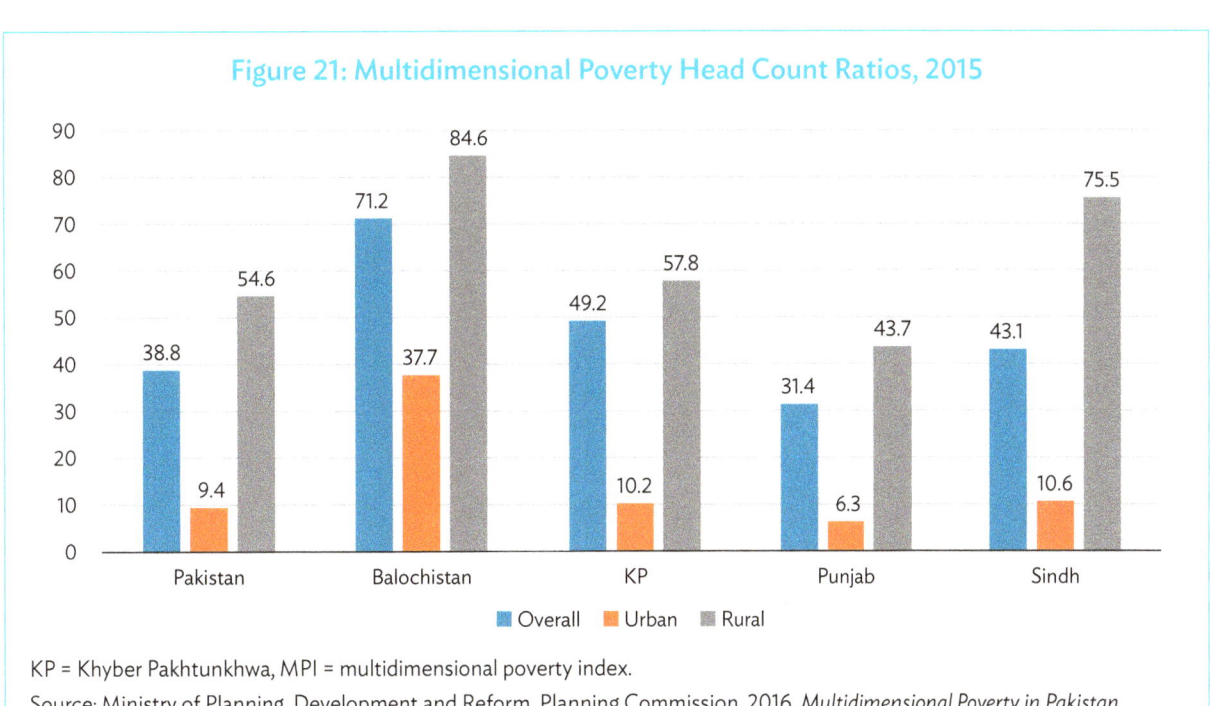

Figure 21: Multidimensional Poverty Head Count Ratios, 2015

KP = Khyber Pakhtunkhwa, MPI = multidimensional poverty index.
Source: Ministry of Planning, Development and Reform. Planning Commission. 2016. *Multidimensional Poverty in Pakistan.*

Using an expanded set of 15 indicators to adapt to Pakistan's context, the MPI database showed deprivations in years of schooling, access to health facilities, and child school attendance as the top contributors to multidimensional poverty in Pakistan.[39] In terms of dimension, deprivations in education were the largest contributor in 2016, followed by living standards, and then health.

A similar MPI profile came out from the Pakistan Social and Living Standards Measurement (PSLM) Survey 2017–2018.[40] It may not have changed significantly until 2020, considering the following results of the PSLM 2019–2020 (footnote 8): (i) urban literacy declined and Pakistan remained in the top three countries with the biggest number of out-of-school children; (ii) health indicators improved at a faster pace even in less developed districts; and (iii) water and sanitation and other standard of living indicators showed progress in some areas but declined in others.

Gender Equality Status and Policy

Gender inequality is deep and persistent in Pakistan. It is evident in all key indicators, such as poverty, education, health, employment, and legal rights. For example, female labor force participation ratio rose steadily from 13.7% in 2000 to 22.22% in 2014 but has fluctuated since 2015 and stood at 21.3% in 2021 (footnote 29). The same indicator for males was 67.9% in 2021. The overall employment rate was 42.1% in 2021, higher in males at 64.1% compared to females at 19.4%.

Women workers tend to be concentrated in the informal sector, agriculture, and home-based work, and as such, receive mostly low and irregular wages.[41] In the formal sector, Pakistani working women are more discriminated against, e.g., in terms of pay, compared to most countries. The International Labour Organization estimated that in 2018,[42] Pakistan's raw gender pay gap was 34.5%, against the world average of 15.8%; its factor-weighted gender pay gap was 36.3% against the world average of 18.8%.[43]

Female literacy rate consistently improved, from 35.4% in 2005 to 51.9% in 2021, but was significantly below the male literacy rate of 64.1% in 2005 and 73.4% in 2021.[44] Although rising consistently, the mean years of schooling among females was less than half that of males in 2005 to 2011. The gap substantially narrowed down in 2019 as female mean years of schooling was recorded at 3.9 years and that of males at 5.0 years.

---

[39] OPHI and UNDP's global multidimensional poverty index comprises 10 standard global indicators, expanded to 15 as recommended by Pakistani authorities. The country indicators now include: (i) education: years of schooling, school attendance, and educational quality; (ii) health: health facilities, immunization, ante-natal care, and assisted delivery; and (iii) living standards: improved walls, overcrowding, electricity, sanitation, cooking fuel, water, assets, and land and livestock (rural). A quantitative deprivation cutoff for each indicator (e.g., years of schooling: deprived if no man OR no woman in the household above 10 years old has completed 5 years of schooling) enables effective monitoring and evaluation and use of MPI as an anti-poverty planning and targeting tool. The World Bank has also developed another set of MPI indicators, adapted to regional (e.g., South Asian, Southeast Asian) contexts to track progress on poverty reduction efforts.
[40] OPHI and UNDP. 2022. *Global Multidimensional Poverty Index 2022. Unpacking Deprivation Bundles to Remove Multidimensional Poverty.* UNDP.
[41] UN Pakistan. 2018. *One United Nations Programme III. 2018–2022. United Nations Sustainable Development Framework for Pakistan.*
[42] The estimates were based on a study of the average (mean) hourly wages in 73 countries covering about 80% of the world's employees. See: International Labour Organization (ILO). 2018. *Global Wage Report 2018/19. What Lies Behind Gender Pay Gaps.*
[43] The raw gender pay gap refers to the difference in pay between women and men at a specific point in time. The factor-weighted gender pay gap adjusts average hourly wage differences by education levels, age, working time (full time versus part time) and status (private sector versus public sector employment).
[44] Government of Pakistan, Finance Division. 2022. *Pakistan Economic Survey 2021–22.*

While official statistics have reported some upward movement in recent years, the country's global ranking in key gender equality indexes remains low. In fact, from being ranked 135th in 2019, Pakistan dropped to 161st of 191 countries in the 2021 UNDP Gender Inequality Index, which measures gender-based disparities across health, empowerment, and the labor market.[45] Besides being the country with the smallest share of women in senior corporate, managerial, and legislative roles, Pakistan landed 145th of 146 countries in 2022 in the World Economic Forum's Global Gender Gap, which measures access to resources and opportunities around the world.[46]

Pakistan is a signatory to several international agreements on gender equality and has adopted numerous laws, policies, and programs to fulfill its commitment to gender equality and women's rights (footnote 44). It needs to fully operationalize this commitment to empower women and enable them to contribute more meaningfully to solving the challenges the country faces.

Urban Governance

Legal Basis

The 18th Amendment provides the overarching legal basis for Pakistan's urban governance framework. Besides strengthening provincial autonomy and jurisdiction on urban affairs, it also put in place Article 140-A, which mandates the devolution by the provinces of political, financial, and administrative powers to elected local governments.[47] Since 2010, all provinces have revised their local government acts (LGAs) but a low commitment to the transfer of funds and functionaries to local governments has undermined decentralized institutions.[48] This has increased rather than decreased the complexity of urban governance, which is riddled with inefficiencies caused by multiple stakeholders with unclear roles and responsibilities, overlapping functions, and competing interests (Figure 22). The powerful legacy of publicly owned providers and the weak transfer of capacity to local governments have deprived elected urban governments of the ability to ensure universal access to high-quality municipal services for their residents.

---

[45] UNDP. Human Development Reports. Gender Inequality Index (GII) (accessed 15 May 2023).
[46] World Economic Forum. 2022. *Insight Report. Global Gender Gap Report 2022*.
[47] I. Ahmed. 2020. The 18th Amendment: Historical Developments and Debates in Pakistan. *ISAS Insights*. National University of Singapore and Institute of South Asian Studies. 4 September. See also: F. Moriani. 2015. The Circularity of Public Policy Reforms in Pakistan: The Case of the 18th Amendment. *Development Advocate Pakistan*. 2 (1).
[48] R. Muhula. 2019. Pakistan@100 Governance & Institutions. *The World Bank Group Policy Note*. World Bank.

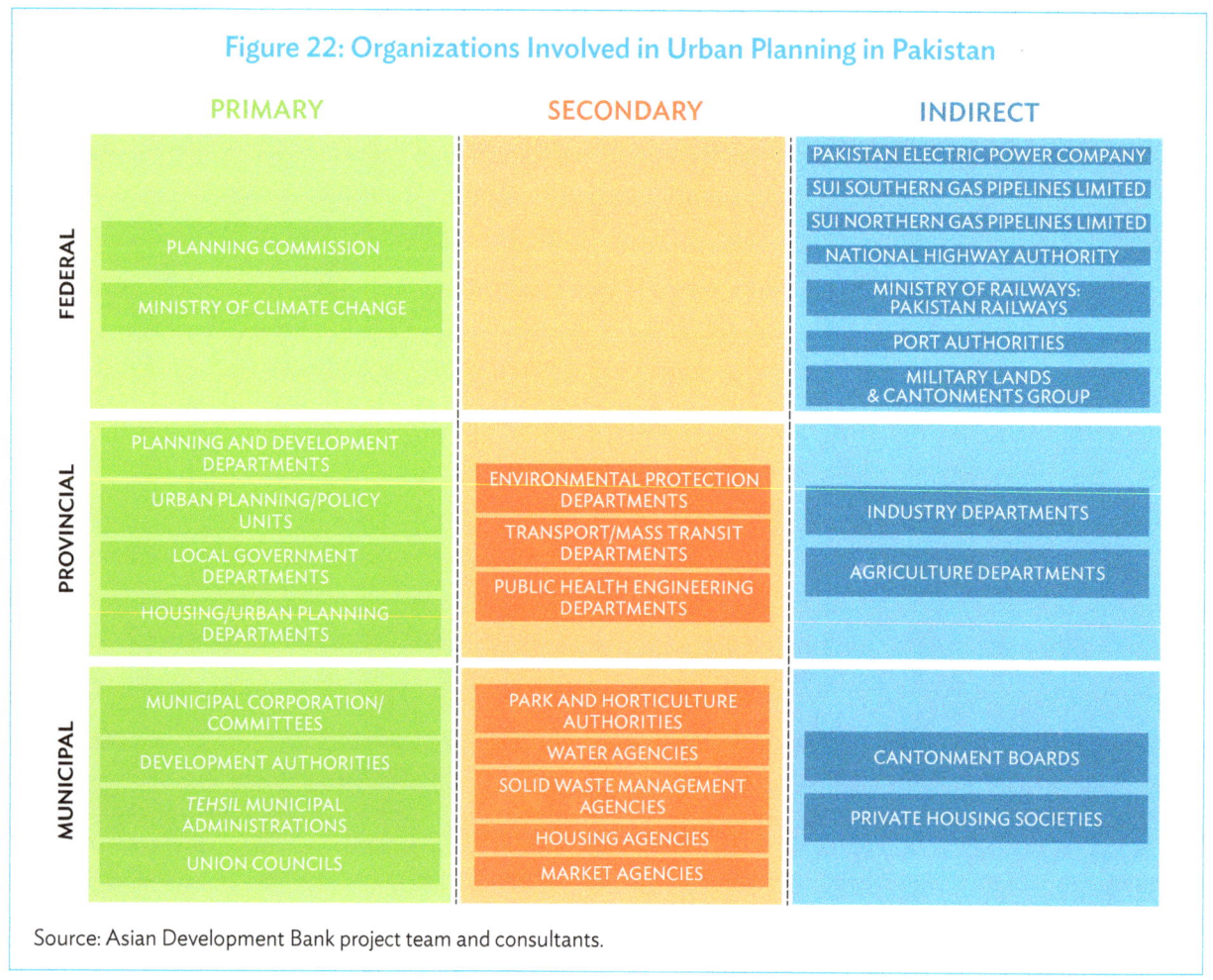

Figure 22: Organizations Involved in Urban Planning in Pakistan

Source: Asian Development Bank project team and consultants.

Institutional Framework: Federal Level

The federal government has had limited involvement in urban governance since the 18th Amendment, except through the Planning Commission and the Ministry of Climate Change, now known as the Ministry of Climate Change and Environmental Coordination (MOCC&EC). However, several other federal institutions, including utility companies, transport agencies, and military departments, impact the country's urban development through their policies and services, by administering urban land and housing, or by executing urban developments.

Planning Commission. Under the supervision of the Ministry of Planning, Development and Reforms, the Planning Commission undertakes research and develops state policies to grow the national economy and expand the country's publicly owned infrastructure. It is chaired by the prime minister, who is assisted by a deputy chair and a science advisor. While most mega infrastructure and urban development projects, especially those funded by international development partners, require concept clearance and approval of the Planning Commission Proforma 1 (PC-1), there is no national policy instrument that provides guidance to the review and approval or disapproval of these urban development projects.[49]

---

[49] PC-1, as referred to in the Planning Commission manual, provides a template for project appraisal and economic analysis of development projects in Pakistan.

Ministry of Climate Change and Environmental Coordination. In 2017, the Ministry of Environment and Urban Affairs was renamed the Ministry of Climate Change and Environmental Coordination (MOCC&EC). The ministry develops national policies, strategies, plans, and programs on climate change and associated sectors and proactively helps provincial governments do the same. It also monitors, ensures implementation, and proposes policy updates and reporting on environmental and related agreements with other countries and international agencies, including the Sustainable Development Goals (SDGs) and the nationally determined contributions (NDCs) under the Paris Agreement. Given the urgency of climate resiliency building, it has become imperative for the MOCC&EC to lessen its reliance on development partners and strengthen its management and business processes to improve efficiencies and enhance policy and program implementation.

Pakistan Electric Power Company. Better known locally as PEPCO, this company was established in 1998 under the Ministry of Energy to implement the strategic plan for commercializing the power wing of the Pakistan Water and Power Development Authority. It manages nine corporatized distribution companies (DISCOs), four generation companies, and the National Transmission and Despatch Company. The DISCOs, responsible for electricity distribution throughout Pakistan except Karachi, have inadvertently facilitated urban sprawl countrywide by providing electricity connections to housing societies without ensuring authorization by the respective development authorities.[50] The practice must be reined in to prevent the further proliferation of poorly planned settlements on city outskirts.

Ministry of Railways. A big portion of the country's urban land is allocated to Pakistan Railways to facilitate the expansion of railways and ancillary structures such as workshops, stations, and marshaling yards. However, much of this land, especially in larger cities, has been infringed upon by formal and informal developments, including encroachments from individual households, which has given rise to many urban slums and unauthorized use by other government departments. In 2015, Pakistan Railways initiated the digitization of its land and other assets to monitor and control encroachment, but this was undermined by the routine unapproved leasing of land by the ministry. The expansion of rail transport networks has given birth to new urban settlements or helped existing rural settlements acquire urban characteristics through improved mobility and access to other areas, thus catalyzing unplanned urbanization in a manner akin to the documented impacts of rail transport expansion in advanced countries.[51]

National Highway Authority. The National Highway Authority has its own Land Management and Infrastructure Wing (LM&IS) that manages the preservation or commercial use of the agency's rights-of-way.[52] Specifically, the LM&IS implements the National Housing Authority's bylaws and policies for the use of rights-of-way for commercial spaces such as gas stations, hotels or motels, restaurants, nurseries, factories, shops, and *khokhas* (kiosks) while prohibiting encroachments and unauthorized residential, infrastructure, and other physical developments. Without recognizing or capturing urban planning boundaries, the land use approval system of the LM&IS has resulted in congested and unplanned city expansions along national corridors. With ribbon urban development emerging along road networks connecting major cities and traversing city boundaries and beyond, it has become ever more important to involve the LM&IS in urban planning processes.

---

[50] Karachi's electricity generation, transmission, and distribution are under K-Electric, a privately owned utility company.
[51] N. Barbopoulos, P. Baltas, and D. Milakis. 2005. *The Impacts of Rail Transit on Urban Sprawl and Mobility of the Western City from Late Ninetieth Century to the Second World War. The Case of London and Los Angeles.* Paper prepared for the Third International Conference, Tourism and the History of Transport, Traffic and Mobility. York. 6–9 October.
[52] National Highway Authority, Road Asset Management Division. 2004. Regulatory Framework and Standard Operating Procedures For Preservation and Commercial Use of Right of Way (ROW)–2002 (Revised 2004).

Port authorities. The Karachi Port Trust, Port Qasim Authority, and Gwadar Port Authority, administered by the Ministry of Maritime Affairs, are responsible for port construction and operation and maintenance (O&M). They own and manage their land independent of the city and provincial governments, which often results in conflicts of interest. The relationship between local governments and these landowning institutions needs to be clarified and reconciled to harmonize urban and port development goals and priorities.[53]

Military departments. Military lands and cantonments do not fall under the jurisdiction of city administrations but are administered by the Military Lands & Cantonments Group, a department attached to the Ministry of Defence. The group oversees the governance of 44 cantonments through the local cantonment boards and manages Ministry of Defence land throughout the country through 11 military estate circles.[54] The cantonment boards are responsible for municipal service delivery within their jurisdiction. Under Cantonment Ordinance 2002, the boards should consult with the civilian administration (i.e., municipal and provincial authorities) on development and planning decisions but are not bound to follow their advice. In practice, such consultations are rarely undertaken, leading to inconsistencies, and even conflicts, in plans and policies between the cantonment boards, the development authorities, and municipal corporations. Given the interdependency of resources and services, this institutional arrangement undermines the optimal use of resources through the integration of urban planning and service provision. Similar independent administration arrangements exist for the land management and real estate activities of the Civil Aviation Authority and the Navy. In contrast to municipal areas, bylaws and regulations are strictly enforced in cantonment areas with almost no encroachment on privately owned lands under their development.

Institutional Framework: Province Level

While most countries have a national urban agenda and/or policy, each province in Pakistan follows its own legislation for municipal-level planning and governance. The provincial and municipal urban governance structures are similar, although there are significant differences between the provinces and cities when it comes to capacity, engagement, and openness for reforms (Figure 23). The definition and use of the terms "urban" and "rural" also vary from province to province.

Three provincial government institutions have a primary role in urban planning: the Planning and Development (P&D) Department or Board, the Local Government Department, and the Housing or Urban Development Planning Department. Three more departments have important but supplementary roles: the Environmental Protection Department, Transport Department, and Public Health Engineering Department (PHED).

Planning and development departments or boards. The P&D department or board is the principal provincial planning organization.[55] It approves provincial plans and budgets and coordinates and monitors the development programs of all departments. It has an economic section or wing that handles the formulation of development plans and strategies, the appraisal and monitoring and evaluation of the development schemes, and coordination with the federal government on economic and policy issues. It also has multiple technical sections or wings that support the work of the economic section and oversees the development and governance activities in the different sectors.

---

[53] A. Hasan et al. 2013. Land Ownership, Control and Contestation in Karachi and Implications for Low-Income Housing. *Urbanization and Emerging Population Issues*. Working Paper 10. International Institute for Environment and Development, Human Settlements Group and United Nations Population Fund.
[54] Government of Pakistan, Military Lands & Cantonments. Ministry of Defence. What We Do.
[55] P&D units are called P&D departments in KP and Balochistan, and P&D boards in Sindh and Punjab.

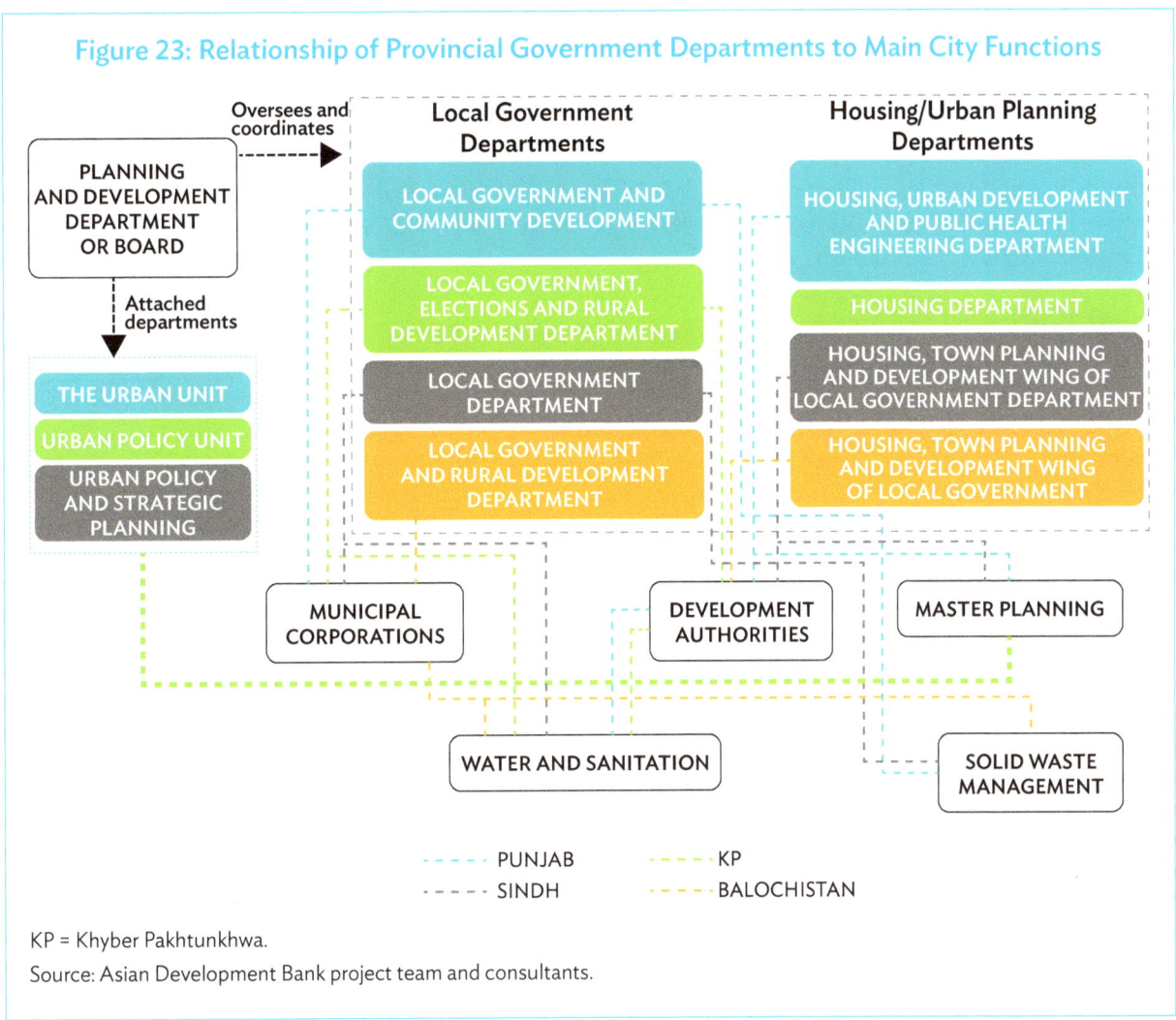

Figure 23: Relationship of Provincial Government Departments to Main City Functions

KP = Khyber Pakhtunkhwa.
Source: Asian Development Bank project team and consultants.

The department's technical wings appraise the proposed projects from different sectors and submit these to the Provincial Development Working Party, the highest approving authority for development projects at the provincial level. The lack of a coherent urban policy and strategy, urban projects have taken a fragmented and piecemeal approach that has done little to curb growing urban challenges. However, the situation could improve with some progress made by the provinces. For example, Punjab and KP have developed provincial spatial strategies, with Punjab also completing regional development plans for select districts and divisions. Balochistan has also prepared a spatial strategy framework document, which may be used as a springboard for developing a more comprehensive urban strategy and policy.

Local government departments. The local government departments have a mandate to implement the LGAs. They also provide administrative support to the various local government tiers and build their capacity to generate revenues, deliver municipal services, and provide infrastructure. All municipal committees and corporations operate under their respective LGAs and the oversight of their elected municipal governments.

In Punjab, the Local Government and Community Development (LG&CD) Department is responsible for the implementation of the Punjab LGA 2022. The LG&CD Department also administers the Punjab Municipal Development Fund Company, solid waste management (SWM) companies, and cattle market management companies operating throughout the province.

In KP, the Local Government, Elections and Rural Development Department implements the 2019 LGA and oversees the Directorate General of the Local Government and Rural Development that administers all village and neighborhood councils, the Local Council Board that administers all municipalities; the Urban Area Development Authorities Board administering the planning and development authorities in the eight large towns; the Provincial Delimitation Authority, administering the boundaries for village and neighborhood committees; and the water and sanitation services companies (WSSCs) that administer water and sanitation services in each divisional capital.[56]

Sindh's Local Government Department ensures the implementation of the Sindh 2013 LGA. It has three wings: the Local Government Wing which oversees the municipal corporations and water and sanitation agencies (WASAs); the Housing Town Planning Wing, overseeing the development authorities and Sindh Building Control Authority; and the Development Wing responsible for implementing, monitoring, and evaluating mega projects in the province.[57]

The Local Government and the Rural Development Department of Balochistan is responsible for implementing the Balochistan LGA 2019. It provides administrative and fiscal support to local councils, including metropolitan corporations, municipal committees, district councils, and union councils.[58]

Housing and urban development, and/or town planning departments. These departments have various functions and mandates, ranging from housing policy to master planning, depending on the province. They usually have several attached agencies and are responsible for the development authorities in most major urban centers. They also act as the link between attached agencies, development authorities, and provincial governments.

In Punjab, the Housing, Urban Development and Public Health Engineering Department administers the Punjab Housing and Town Planning Agency, the development authorities and WASAs in major cities, the parks and horticulture authorities, and the PHED. It has many functions, covering housing, master planning, municipal services delivery, horticulture development, and maintenance of public spaces.

Compared with its counterpart in Punjab, the mandate of the Housing Department of KP and its only field arm, the Provincial Housing Authority, is limited. The department's primary function is to facilitate the provision of housing units or land for housing to low-income public and government employees. The formulation of provincial land use policies and plans, preparation of regional development plans and inter-district spatial planning, support to federal government in land use and development plan implementation, and development of geographic information systems for land registry and information related to town and urban planning also fall within its purview. However, little or no implementation is yet reported on these responsibilities.[59]

---

[56] Government of Khyber Pakhtunkhwa. Local Government, Elections and Rural Development Department. Functions.
[57] Local Government Department. Government of Sindh. Wings of Local Government Department (under development as of press time).
[58] Government of Balochistan. Local Government Department.
[59] Government of Khyber Pakthunkhwa. Provincial Housing Authority.

In Sindh, the Housing Town Planning Wing of the Local Government Department has a similar role. It oversees the Sindh Building Control Authority, the Directorate of Town Planning, and development authorities. The Government of Sindh is in the process of developing the Sindh Urban and Regional Master Plan Authority, which will be responsible for urban master planning in the province.

In Balochistan, the Urban Planning and Development Department has a mandate to take charge of master planning in urban centers and oversees the development authorities.

Environmental protection and climate change agencies. The provincial environmental protection and climate change departments, functioning under the Pakistan Environmental Protection Act and the Climate Change Act 2017, are responsible for protecting and improving the environment, promoting sustainable development, and assessing and monitoring the impacts of climate change. Common areas of focus are air, water, soil, and noise pollution; climate change; and SWM.

Punjab's Environmental Protection Agency screens development projects for environmental impact, but has a narrow regulatory scope and lacks enforcement power.[60] In 2021, the Sindh Environmental, Climate Change and Coastal Development Agency completed the preparation of the province's climate change policy, focusing on building the resilience of the coastal ecosystem and ensuring a healthy urban environment.[61] KP's Environmental Protection and Climate Change Agency set up vehicle emission testing stations among its initial initiatives.[62] The Balochistan Environmental Protection and Climate Change Agency, operating under the Balochistan Environmental Protection Act, 2012 and the Climate Change Act, 2017, enforces quantitative and qualitative standards to abate air, water, soil, and noise pollution.[63]

Transport and mass transit departments. Provincial transport departments take charge of transport legislation, regulation, policy, and planning.

The Punjab Provincial Transport Authority, attached to the Transport Department of Punjab, presides over district regional transport authorities to smooth the implementation of policies throughout the province. A specialized body, the Punjab Masstransit Authority, plans, regulates, and oversees the construction and operation of the mass transit systems, outsourcing most of the systems' O&M requirements to the private sector.[64] The Lahore Transport Company, established under Section 42 of the Companies Ordinance, 1984, primarily ensures the smooth functioning of the transport system in the city outside the mass transit corridors.[65]

Several authorities are attached to the Transport and Mass Transit Department of Sindh, mandated to construct and maintain the mass transit systems in the province. These include the Sindh Mass Transit Authority, Karachi Public Transport Authority, Sindh Road Transport Corporation, and TransKarachi, a Section 42 company that operates the mass transit systems in Karachi. As in other provinces, the regional transport authorities take charge of planning the public transport routes, including the location of ancillary structures such as terminals and taxi stands, and the licensing of public transport vehicles at the city level.

---

[60] Government of the Punjab. Environment Protection and Climate Change Department. Overview.
[61] Government of Sindh. Environment, Climate Change and Coastal Development Department. About Us.
[62] Government of Khyber Pakhtunkhwa. Environmental Protection Agency.
[63] Government of Balochistan. Balochistan Environmental Protection Agency.
[64] Government of the Punjab. Punjab Masstransit Authority.
[65] A nonprofit company is registered under Section 42 of the Companies Ordinance, 1984 as a public company with limited liability provided it directs or intends to direct its profits or any other form of income to advancing public sector objectives.

In 2008, the Government of KP established a separate transport department to administer the province's Directorate of Transport, Provincial Transport Authority, district and regional transport authorities, and Road Transport Board.[66] Recently, a business development unit was formed in the Transport Department of KP. It functions as a planning wing and monitors developmental schemes. A transport planning and engineering unit was also created to address transport issues through scientific innovation. The Government of KP has established the KP Urban Mobility Authority to plan and regulate the mass transit system in the province. TransPeshawar, a Section 42 company, operates the mass transit system in Peshawar mainly through outsourcing.

Urban mobility regulations and institutional frameworks have improved in Punjab and KP over the last 10 years. But Sindh's transition is at an early stage, while Balochistan has not yet started. Overlapping mandates and jurisdictions, causing transport planning and management inefficiencies, have persisted and need to be eradicated.

There is a broad consensus in all provinces on the need for an integrated planning framework for sustainable urban mobility that brings together all modes of transport, both motorized and nonmotorized. However, the development of this planning framework is yet to commence.

Public health engineering departments. Provincial PHEDs primarily design and build water supply and sanitation facilities for underserved rural areas. In most cases, PHEDs provide advice and technical support to the rural local governments, communities, and households that are responsible for the ownership and O&M of these assets. While the functions of the PHED are common to all provinces, their line department varies from province to province.

Urban planning and policy units. The lack of capacity for analyzing urbanization trends and modeling urban scenarios under different policy instruments is a major constraint among provincial governments. Similarly, the lack of capacity for developing well-researched multisector spatial plans (master plans, land use plans, and reclassification plans) and the elaboration of well-defined development needs for each subsector is a major constraint among local governments.

To address these constraints, the P&D Board of Punjab established its Urban Unit to conduct research and analysis on urbanization. To date, the Urban Unit has been involved in almost every aspect of urban analysis, modeling, and planning throughout the province. Today, the Urban Unit is a provincial government-owned corporate entity, employing qualified professionals at market rates and generating annual returns for the province. While the Urban Unit could be engaged by municipal governments or development authorities for city master planning, the reality is that the Urban Unit is almost exclusively engaged by provincial government departments.

In KP, the P&D Department established its Urban Policy and Planning Unit as the principal organization for undertaking urban planning on behalf of the *tehsils* throughout the province. It has also delegated to the unit the urban development authorities in the province's eight major towns. While the delivery of spatial plans by the provincial government is more likely to facilitate provincial funding for their implementation by the provincial departments, it does not align with the assignment of responsibilities to the *tehsils* and neighborhood councils for spatial planning.

In Sindh, the Directorate of Urban Policy and Strategic Planning within the P&D Department exercises responsibility for urban planning. This contradicts the mandate of local governments to prepare, implement, and regulate spatial plans (i.e., master plans, land use plans, and land classification and/or reclassification). The weak capacity of local governments and lack of incentives to implement the spatial plans prepared by the provincial government is a major challenge in Sindh.

---

[66] Government of Khyber Pakhtunkhwa. Transport and Mass Transit Development Projects.

Institutional Framework: Municipal Level

Since 2010, the local governments in all provinces have gradually moved from a three-tier system of councils at the district, subdistrict or municipality, and union level to a two-tier system. This has variously combined the district council focus on agriculture, community development, education, and health with the subdistrict[67] or town council focus on municipal infrastructure services; and in most cases, retained the union council or village and/or neighborhood committee focus on community-based services.[68]

Under the Balochistan LGA 2010, all urban jurisdictions are governed separately from rural jurisdictions. Urban dwellers are represented by a single-tier local government system where residents directly elect their ward member, who represents their interests on the municipal committee, municipal corporation, or metropolitan corporation. Rural dwellers are represented by a two-tier local government system where residents directly elect their ward member, who then elects their union council chair, who represents their interests on the district council.[69]

Under the Sindh LGA 2013, all urban jurisdictions are governed separately from rural jurisdictions. Urban dwellers in metropolitan corporations are represented by a three-tier local government system where residents directly elect their ward committee member and their union committee chair and vice chair, who then represent their interests in both the metropolitan corporation and the town municipal corporation. Urban dwellers in municipal corporations are represented by a two-tier local government system, where residents directly elect their ward member, who then elects their town or municipal committee chair. This chair also represents their interests in the municipal corporation. Rural dwellers are represented by a two-tier local government system where residents directly elect their ward member and their union council chair and vice chair, as well as their district council member, who represent their interests on the district council.[70]

Under the KP LGA 2019, all urban and rural dwellers are represented by a single two-tier governance structure where residents directly elect their neighborhood or village council member, who then elects a chair to represent their interests on the *tehsil*.[71]

Under the Punjab LGA 2022, all urban jurisdictions are governed separately from rural jurisdictions, although all urban and rural dwellers are represented by the same two-tier governance structure, with residents directly electing their urban or rural council member, who then elects a chair to represent them on either the metropolitan corporation (urban) or the district council (rural).[72]

The administration of cantonments is expressly excluded from the LGAs. The governance of cantonments is the responsibility of the cantonment boards comprising primarily military-appointed staff with residents represented by directly elected members.

---

[67] A subdistrict is generally referred to as a *tehsil* in Pakistan. In Sindh province, it is called a *taluka*.
[68] Commonwealth Local Government Forum. *The Local Government System in Pakistan. Country Profile 2017-18.*
[69] Election Commission of Pakistan. *Handbook for Returning Officers. Local Government Election—2022 Balochistan.*
[70] Election Commission of Pakistan. *Handbook for District Returning Officers. Local Government Election—2022 Sindh.*
[71] Election Commission of Pakistan. *Handbook for Returning Officers. Local Government Election—2021 Khyber Pakhtunkhwa.*
[72] Government of the Punjab. The Punjab Local Government Act 2022 (Act XXXIII of 2022).

Urban municipal institutions. Most of the larger urban centers have a local development authority tasked with planning and managing urban land use and established in parallel to an elected municipal committee or corporation responsible for the delivery of municipal services. The relationship between the local development authorities and elected municipal governments has been muddled by legacy structures with divergent reporting and supervision systems.

In Punjab, while the LGA 2013 placed the development authorities under the responsibility of elected metropolitan corporations (city governments), they are established in major urban centers as corporate bodies reporting administratively to the province's Housing Department. These development authorities are managed by the *nazim* (city administrator), appointed at the discretion of the provincial government as chair of the board of their respective corporate entities. This neither results in the clear delegation of service responsibility from the metropolitan corporation to the development authority nor does it shield the development authority from undue political influence.

In KP, the Urban Areas Development Authorities Act (2020) established local authorities in major urban centers as corporate entities responsible for urban planning and development activities and reporting administratively to the Urban Development Authorities' Board.[73] On the other hand, the KP LGA 2019 assigned responsibility for spatial planning (including land use and zoning) and the regulation and implementation of these plans to municipal governments. The disconnect between these two legal mandates seems to have not been resolved by the Urban Policy 2030, which set the development of indicative strategic city management plans as a joint responsibility of the district and municipal governments, with their approval to be made by the District Land Use and Management Committee.[74]

The Balochistan Development Authority Act (1974) established the Balochistan Development Authority within the P&D Department to administratively oversee the Quetta Development Authority, created as a corporate body in 1974, and the Gwadar Development Authority, created as a similar body in 2003. Both bodies are mandated to prepare, implement, and regulate master plans for their respective areas. This mandate needs to be reconciled with that under the Balochistan LGA 2010, which unambiguously assigns master planning, zoning, and land use control to the municipal government councils.

In Sindh's major urban centers, local development authorities have been established as corporate entities in charge of developing and implementing master plans under the administrative guidance of the Housing Town Planning Wing of the provincial Local Government Department. However, the Sindh LGA 2013 has simultaneously assigned the responsibility for master plans, site development schemes, and building control to metropolitan corporations, municipal committees, or town committees. With the reduction in local government resources and a trend toward centralization of administrative control over urban planning and services, the municipal service structures have tended to be more fragmented and unwieldy in the larger urban centers.

Devolution challenge. Local elections to facilitate the devolution of urban governance following the 18th Amendment were completed only in 2015. Subsequent elections were postponed due to census-related constitutional issues and the COVID-19 pandemic. In 2021, no cities or municipalities in Pakistan had any elected officials, and until late-2022 were all run by provincial government appointees. While Balochistan, KP, and Sindh now have elected local officials, the prolonged interregnum experienced by all provinces reveals the tendency of the LGAs "to subordinate the local governments to the provincial governments, despite Article 140-A … " (footnote 48, p.26).

---

[73] The Khyber Pakhtunkhwa Urban Areas Development Authorities Act 2020.
[74] Government of Khyber Pakhtunkhwa, Policy and Planning Department, Urban Policy and Planning Unit. 2022. *Khyber Pakhtunkhwa Urban Policy 2030*.

Nevertheless, some support for devolution may be built upon, including KP's abolition of the district councils and subsequent shift to a two-tier governance system and the establishment of neighborhood and village committees in urban and rural areas under its LGA 2019. Similarly, the Punjab LGA 2022 has devolved public service delivery functions to the district councils or metropolitan corporations and assigned the responsibility for municipal service provision in the province's 11 major urban agglomerations to locally elected metropolitan corporations. Furthermore, under the act, all the development authorities, WASAs, parks and horticulture authorities, traffic engineering and planning agencies, and waste management companies are to be either administered or engaged by municipal local governments.

However, in Sindh, there is a tendency to centralize services, including those previously decentralized. For example, while Sindh's LGA 2013 assigned master planning to metropolitan corporations, municipal committees, or town committees, the provincial government simultaneously strengthened the master planning capacity of the province's Directorate of Urban Policy and Strategic Planning. This centralization trend, which arises from tensions between the political parties that control the provincial government and the local governments of Karachi and Hyderabad, highlights how political dynamics can undermine effective governance.

Lessons in decentralization. KP's experience in decentralization, the most advanced among the provinces, highlights two important lessons. First, while decentralization impacts the urban sector positively, improvements can be slow as cities expand rapidly, and available resources fail to meet demand. Second, increased allocations to support decentralization need to consider absorptive capacity to optimize their use by the local governments.

In KP's case, decentralization has led to better sanitation services, increased awareness, and better response to people's complaints, among other benefits. However, KP's decision to allocate directly to local governments 30% of the funding for its provincial annual development plan (ADP), regarded by many as the real breakthrough in the provincial decentralization process, was eroded to 22% in FY2018 due to underutilization, alleged inefficiency, and lack of absorptive capacity.[75] This underscores the imperative to engage in local capacity building as a cornerstone of effective decentralization.

Need for interprovincial coordination. This assessment acknowledges that urban affairs is a provincial and local government subject in Pakistan's context. However, the variations in the local government model and the degree of decentralization implemented by the provinces may indicate the need for a mechanism to coordinate the devolution process. The coordination mechanism could address the inconsistencies in the tenure of local governments and local electoral processes, which impact the pace and continuity of reforms and the effectiveness and viability of decentralization under the 18th Amendment.

Urban Planning

Legal and Policy Framework

Pakistan formulated its national urban policy in 2011.[76] However there has been no impetus for the policy's implementation in the absence of a federal anchor to coordinate the urban sector following the 18th Amendment.

Provinces exercise responsibility for land management, including analyzing urbanization growth trends and risks, producing regional spatial plans, and developing incentives for sustainable municipal services. The provinces have variously delegated the responsibility for urban planning to local governments through their LGAs. In general,

---

[75] S.M. Ali. 2018. *Devolution of Power in Pakistan*. United States Institute of Peace. Special Report 422. March.
[76] Government of Pakistan, Planning Commission. 2011. *Task Force Report on Urban Development*.

the LGAs assign the responsibility for the preparation, approval, and enforcement of spatial plans, master plans, zoning, and land use plans, including classification and reclassification of land, urban design, and urban renewal to local governments. Local governments are also empowered to approve land use plans and enforce them through bylaws, especially in areas lacking a master plan, allowing even rural local governments to regulate land use in urbanizing areas to ensure access to municipal services in these areas. In larger cities, some of these functions have been assigned, via provincial government orders, acts, and ordinances, to development authorities or planning agencies. These include the Karachi Development Authority Order (1957), the Capital Development Authority Ordinance (1960), the Lahore Development Authority Act (1975), the Quetta Development Authority Act (1978), and the Gwadar Development Authority Act (2003). While all these local development authorities were placed under district governments under the 2001 Local Government Ordinance, this did not significantly improve the performance of the local development authorities.

Master planning activities commenced in Pakistan with the initiation of the Greater Lahore Master Plan in 1961, followed by the preparation of Karachi's Master Plan between 1970 and 1974. Master plans were subsequently developed for other cities such as Quetta, Peshawar, Rawalpindi, Faisalabad, and Multan, often with external assistance. Between 1960 and 1980, urban planning primarily emphasized comprehensive land use planning, leading to the formulation of master, land use, and zoning plans. From 1980 to 2000, the approach shifted toward drafting long-term, policy-driven documents like outline development plans and structure plans. In 2001, the term "spatial plan" was adopted to describe various urban planning strategies. With the introduction of the Punjab Land Use Rules in 2009,[77] urban planning practice has expanded to include peri-urban plans and land use classification or reclassification plans.

Punjab

In Punjab, the responsibility for the preparation, approval, and enforcement of master plans primarily lies with the local governments. In larger cities, this responsibility is exercised by local development authorities. The Punjab LGA 2022 stipulates that elected metropolitan corporations or district councils may delegate some of their planning and development functions to these authorities; however, these development authorities, established under provincial legislation, operate largely independently of the city governance structure. The Punjab Housing and Town Planning Agency supports urbanization analysis provincially while also preparing detailed spatial plans for urban local governments. Urban planning is also supported by the Urban Unit, a provincial government-owned corporate entity that provides urban planning services on a fee-for-service basis.

Punjab's Spatial Strategy 2047 focuses on regulating urban land use based on outputs, such as contribution to social and economic value of an area.[78] This spatial strategy is built around the Punjab Growth Strategy 2023, the latest version of the province's comprehensive development plan. It is less prescriptive than the earlier Punjab Spatial Strategy 2016–2040, which prioritized the location of municipal infrastructure investments (especially transport networks) necessary to boost economic growth, including industrial estates and large-scale infrastructure projects.

---

[77] Government of Punjab, Local Government and Community Development Department. 2009. *Notification: No. SOR (LG) 38-18/2009.* 27 June.
[78] Government of the Punjab, Urban Unit, and World Bank. 2017. *Punjab Spatial Strategy 2047. A Framework for Integrated Spatial Planning and Sustainable Development.*

In 2021, the LG&CD Department of Punjab launched a project to develop Master Land Use Plans for *tehsils*, which aim to map out urban growth, formulate master plans, and develop policies for improved service delivery and capacity building in 11 districts in the first phase and 23 districts in the second phase, out of a total of 36 districts. The planning process has involved district planning and development committees led by the Deputy Commissioner and Municipal Officer of Planning. These also serve as a collaborative platform for stakeholder consultations to incorporate diverse local insights and expertise. To date, 145 out of the 257 declared urban areas in the province have an approved spatial plan.

Khyber Pakhtunkhwa

The province's LGA assigns land use zoning and master planning to the *tehsils*, including classification and reclassification of land and the creation of their respective bylaws. In practice, however, it is the Urban Policy and Planning Unit of the P&D Department that undertakes urban planning on behalf of the *tehsils* throughout the province.

The Khyber Pakhtunkhwa Urban Policy 2030 (footnote 74) outlines the province's goals and indicators on land use, housing, economic and real estate development, municipal services, tourism, capacity building, and other areas of urban development. Building on a comprehensive assessment of KP's urban sector, it recommends the application of the urban policy to three zones, consisting of mainly urban areas, contiguous non-urban areas, and rapidly urbanizing areas.

The policy emphasizes the development of master plans and their implementation through the formulation of strategic city management plans on a 3-year rolling basis. The process for developing the strategic plans is well-defined and structured to ensure that it is participatory. These plans are to be developed collaboratively by the deputy commissioner of the district, the mayor or chair of the city, and the director general of any relevant development authority, with the chief executive officer of the applicable cantonment board(s) to be consulted wherever possible. These plans will then need approval from the District Land Use and Management Committee.

The land use plans crafted at the city level will serve as a guide for the detailed and legally binding land use plans that are to be developed at the neighborhood council level. The initial action in reviewing any applications for land use change or reclassification will require a comprehensive environmental impact assessment. This assessment will cover the implications for traffic, water, and sanitation, evaluating the current and future conditions, and shall be accomplished by an independent, qualified consulting firm in partnership with the Environmental Protection Agency.

Balochistan

Balochistan's LGA has assigned "land use control, zoning, master planning, classification, declassification, or reclassification of commercial or residential areas, markets, housing, urban or rural infrastructure, environment and construction, maintenance or development thereof" to local government councils. Town planning is a compulsory function of urban councils but any local council "may, within the area of its jurisdiction, with prior approval of Government, frame projects for Town Improvement and constitute a Town Improvement Committee for the purpose."[79]

---

[79] Balochistan Provincial Assembly Secretariat. 2010. *The Balochistan Local Government Act, 2010 (Act No. V of 2010)*.

In practice, the Department of Urban Planning and Development serves as the principal entity overseeing urban growth within Balochistan. To carry out its framework for the development of a provincial spatial strategy, Balochistan has embarked on a program to establish a databank to help streamline public investment planning, align it more closely with pressing development needs, and identify priority development sectors.[80]

The Balochistan Town Planning and Building Rules 2021 cover the certification and approval of building projects, adherence to professional standards, material testing requirements, and urban management of space in streets, roads, and buildings. These rules are compliant with the Pakistan Building Code 2007, particularly regarding seismic safety measures, street width requirements, emergency access, and building height limitations.

Despite these various urban planning regulations, noncompliance is widespread. The spread of unregistered development and inadequate management of roads, waste, sanitation, and lighting highlight the weaknesses in urban planning and governance across Balochistan. The reluctance to enforce town planning rules and steep limitations in local government capacities present a fundamental challenge to managing urban development in Balochistan.

Sindh

Although it has sector policies and plans on drinking water supply, sanitation, and transport, Sindh has no overarching policy to guide urban planning and development. The province's LGA 2013 assigned town planning functions (of master planning and site development schemes) and building control functions (of erection, completion, and regulation of buildings) to the metropolitan corporation, municipal committee, or town committees.[81] In parallel, the Government of Sindh has centralized significant urban development capacities, even transferring lesser local body departments such as sanitation to the Sindh Solid Waste Management Board.

A similar trend is happening at the Directorate of Urban Policy and Strategic Planning in the P&D Department, which develops master plans for local governments. To date, the directorate has prepared master plans for 17 towns and/or secondary cities, although the Defence Housing Authority and cantonment boards continue to operate independently of these master plans. This disjunct between the local responsibility for the preparation and regulation of urban plans versus the centralization of the capacity for their preparation needs to be reconciled.

Municipal Finances

Revenue Sources and Uses

Inadequate municipal finances are a significant obstacle facing the cities. Under current arrangements, cities can collect local taxes and fees, including parking fees, entertainment taxes, licenses and permits, and rental of property assets like municipal markets. Some development authorities collect revenues by auctioning residential and commercial plots on new housing developments. However, city sales tax and property tax are collected by the provincial governments. Personal and corporate income taxes, the bulk of the government's tax revenues, go straight to the federal government along with other major taxes, such as the general sales tax or value-added tax, federal excise duty, and customs duties.

---

[80] Consortium for Development Policy Research. 2021. *A Framework for Development of Balochistan Spatial Strategy*.
[81] UN Environment Programme and Law and Environment Assessment Platform, Montevideo Law Environmental Programme. Sindh Local Government Act, 2013 (Act XLII of 2013).

City tax collections are used mainly to cover part of operational costs, not the development or improvement of services and infrastructure. Consequently, urban authorities have limited finances and rely on budget transfers from the provinces and the federal government to invest in infrastructure and deliver essential urban services.[82]

Important development projects such as the Green Line bus rapid transit in Karachi are directly funded by the federal government and implemented through federal agencies. Centrally collected income and other direct taxes are returned partially to the local governments based on the province's allocation formula. Funds for infrastructure and services are allocated through the provincial governments, mainly the P&D and housing departments. Development budgets are prepared as part of the ADP. Pakistan's budget allocation systems are discussed in the Appendix.

Due to limited funding, holistic and integrated planning is not executed, and only piecemeal development occurs. Lack of funding is an important reason why cities are mostly unable to implement their plans. Moreover, the long-standing reliance on allocations from the provincial and federal governments has reinforced the patron–client tradition in local governance and disincentivized urban authorities from developing investments and exploring opportunities to increase their revenue base and financial capacity.

Revenue Opportunities

Revenue opportunities vary among cities. Big cities have significant revenue sources, and this is reflected in the 95% contribution of the 10 major cities to federal tax revenue in 2018, with Karachi alone accounting for 55% of this federal revenue (footnote 35). Revenue sources of intermediate and small cities are obviously much less.

Despite the capacity and willingness of some consumers to pay for improved services, government subsidies for water supply, sewerage, waste collection, etc., make these services almost free in most cities. This has developed a corresponding mindset among citizens, making it difficult for publicly owned utilities to implement user charges and other cost-recovery schemes. As a result, they have become reliant on government subsidies for much of their O&M costs. The arrangement has drained public coffers and posed a risk to the financial sustainability of utilities and the continued improvement of municipal services. The lack of financial sustainability of public utilities is generally acknowledged, for example by Punjab, which has reported in one of its technical papers substantiating its recently completed spatial strategy that all its service utilities are not even in a break-even position.[83]

There is an untapped potential in most cities' local taxation and revenue collection schemes. The Punjab Spatial Strategy 2047 (footnote 78) has highlighted these issues to include widespread billing and collection inefficiencies, wide-ranging property tax exemptions, poor utilization of revenue-generating public assets, and weak urban property taxation and urban land valuation. Major cities in other provinces also apparently encounter these issues. For example, Sindh's urban property tax revenue is four times lower than that of Punjab.[84] Punjab is

---

[82] These funds are allocations from the divisible pool of tax and nontax revenue collections that go directly to the federal government and are plowed back to the provinces based solely on population size as of 1996. Called the National Finance Commission awards and the Provincial Finance Commission awards, the inclusion of other criteria and the creation of other types of allocations and/or grants complicated the process of determining the provincial allocations or awards from the divisible pool. Thus, instead of being reviewed and updated every 5 years, the allocation formula has not been updated since 1996. The last time the provincial governments had a consensus on the formula was in 2009. See: State Bank of Pakistan. 2010. Special Section 2. National Finance Commission Awards – A Review. *The State of Pakistan's Economy*. First Quarterly Report for FY10.
[83] Government of the Punjab. Undated. Technical Paper 12. Municipal Services. In *Punjab Spatial Strategy 2047*.
[84] World Bank. 2018. *Transforming Karachi into a Livable and Competitive Megacity: A City Diagnostic and Transformation Strategy*. Directions in Development—Infrastructure.

currently developing policy proposals to address these issues. Meanwhile, the province is focusing on digitization and capacity building to reduce system inefficiencies; promote accountability, transparency, and professionalism; and reward good performance in revenue collection—through programs such as the IT [information technology]-Based Monitoring System, Punjab Cities Program, and Punjab Municipal Services Program.

The empowerment of local governments is directly related to financial and administrative devolution. The issues of capacity and revenue generation are interlinked (footnote 75). An increased capacity in local governments will enable them to strengthen their revenue base and, in turn, enhance their financial capacity, planning, and services provision.

Safety and Security

Safety and security have been major issues for most cities in Pakistan in the last few decades. The prolonged instability in neighboring Afghanistan[85] has significantly contributed to higher costs of doing business and economic losses in Pakistan. Between 2001 and 2017, estimates place the cost to Pakistan due to terrorism incidents at approximately $123 billion.[86] The impact was significant in all economic sectors. Foreign investments dried up, international experts avoided Pakistan, the pace of privatization programs slowed down, and exports plummeted.

Of 141 economies, Pakistan ranked 126th in the security indicator of the World Economic Forum's 2019 Global Competitiveness Index and last in the terrorism incidence sub-indicator (footnote 35). The threat of terrorism has been greater in Balochistan and KP. Crime and sectarian violence are a significant concern in Karachi. Violent extremism, street crimes, and the growth of illicit trades are the main reasons mixed housing schemes give way to segregated ethnic and sectarian neighborhoods, with people feeling more secure in being surrounded by their community. Besides the prospect of better municipal services, this also explains why there is a high demand for housing in private gated societies from upper-income groups.

In the last few years, the safety situation has improved in most parts of the country due to the security and anti-terrorism operations carried out by the federal and provincial governments. The security problem is acknowledged in Pakistan Vision 2025, which seeks to establish "a link between development and peace where peace becomes an essential outcome of the development projects." The Ministry of Planning, Development and Special Initiatives (now Ministry of Planning, Development and Reforms) has set up the Peace and Development Unit "not only to raise awareness on the subject, [and] integrate peace and stability as one of the [key performance indicators] of development projects, but also conduct research and assessment studies on peace and conflict in the country for policymakers and public."

Cultural Heritage and Tourism

Tourism is significantly underdeveloped in Pakistan due to limited infrastructure, safety concerns, and, in some cases, negligence of cultural heritage. Pakistan Vision 2025 recognizes the sector's potential and the institutional efforts needed to preserve, train, and promote the country's diverse tourist attractions and improve its international image.

---

[85] ADB placed on hold its regular assistance in Afghanistan effective 15 August 2021.
[86] Government of Pakistan, Finance Division. 2017. Annex-IV Impact of War in Afghanistan and Ensuing Terrorism on Pakistan's Economy. *Pakistan Economic Survey 2016-17*.

Around 400 cultural sites are under the protection of the Federal Department of Archaeology. In addition, each province has named its cultural sites. The Punjab Special Premises (Preservation) Ordinance 1985 has listed 272 sites, the Sindh Cultural Heritage (Preservation) Act 1994 has 1,600 sites, KP has 85 cultural heritage sites, and Balochistan has 28 protected and 57 unprotected sites. Apart from these, hundreds of other sites have not been listed or protected despite their historical and architectural merit (footnote 35).

Six cultural sites are included in the United Nations Educational, Scientific and Cultural Organization (UNESCO) World Heritage list: (i) archaeological ruins at Moenjodaro; (ii) Taxila archaeological site; (iii) Buddhist ruins of Takht-i-Bahi and neighboring city remains at Sahr-i-Bahlol; (iv) Fort and Shalimar Gardens in Lahore; (v) historical monuments at Makli, Thatta; and (vi) Rohtas Fort. Twenty-six more sites are on the tentative list for nomination.[87]

Despite significant historical and cultural resources, visitors in most large cities go for business and health reasons. In many cases, built heritage is unrecognized and under constant threat of encroachment by urban development. Significant investment is needed in infrastructure, heritage preservation, and safety to allow tourism to flourish and contribute to the urban economy. However, none of the large cities can set a long-term tourism strategy on its own, and this sector's near-term development has minimal prospects.

---

[87] UNESCO. World Heritage Convention. Properties Inscribed on the World Heritage List: Pakistan.

Climate Assessment

Background

Pakistan is a blend of various landscapes, ranging from the glaciers, snowcapped mountains, forests, plateaus, plains, and deserts of the Karakoram mountains and Hindu Khush Himalayan ranges in the north to the coastal areas of the Arabian Sea in the south. The Indus River and its many tributaries traverse the entire country, supporting almost 90% of its population.[88] Mismanagement of the river system has led to its degradation, resulting in reduced ground cover, excessive runoff, and increased intensity and severity of floods downstream. Climate change-induced, above-average temperatures in the upper watersheds have accelerated glacial melt and increased the risk of dangerous glacial lake outburst floods (GLOFs). GLOFs have caused the loss of lives and property in remote and impoverished mountain communities and urban areas downstream.[89]

Climate Change and Disaster Risks

In 2022, Pakistan suffered among the worst floods in its history. Caused by the heaviest and most concentrated monsoon rains ever recorded, the floods starkly exhibited the escalation of climate and disaster risks and concomitant economic and social costs to the country.[90] Some 33 million people were affected. More than 1,730 lives were lost. About 8 million people were displaced, and around 2 million houses were damaged or destroyed. Stretches of roads were washed away, dams and water supply systems wrecked, 22,000 schools were damaged and closed for some time, and a near-complete loss of livestock and *kharif* (summer crops) smashed the livelihoods of many.[91]

The total $30 billion estimated economic damage and losses from the 2022 floods was three times the $10 billion of costs incurred by the 2010 floods, then deemed as the most catastrophic in Pakistan's history.[92] It equated to an 8% GDP loss in 2022, with spillover effects amounting to a 2.2% GDP decline in 2023.[93] The 2022 floods represented 80% of the total cost of all other major flood events in the country's history.[94]

The 2010 and 2022 floods combined killed more than 3,700 people (footnote 93). In 2015, Pakistan's deadliest heat wave, reaching 49°C, killed some 1,200 people in Karachi alone, while droughts, whose impacts take time to unfold, brought down the average GDP growth from 6.0% to 2.6% between 2000 and 2002 and heightened the

---

[88] Food and Agriculture Organization of the United Nations (FAO). 2011. *AQUASTAT Transboundary River Basins—Indus River Basin*.
[89] UNDP Pakistan. Scaling-Up of Glacial Lake Outburst Flood (GLOF) Risk Reduction in Northern Pakistan.
[90] World Bank Group. 2022. *Country Climate and Development Report. Pakistan. South Asia*.
[91] World Bank. 2022. Pakistan: Flood Damages and Economic Losses Over USD 30 Billion and Reconstruction Needs Over USD 16 Billion—New Assessment. News release. 28 October.
[92] World Bank Group and Asian Development Bank. 2021. *Climate Risk Country Profile: Pakistan*.
[93] Government of Pakistan, MCC&EC. 2023. *National Adaptation Plan: Pakistan 2023*.
[94] Government of Pakistan, Ministry of Water Resources, Office of the Chief Engineering Adviser and Chairman, Federal Flood Commission. 2022. *Annual Report 2021*.

prevalence of acute and chronic malnutrition, leading to significant upticks in children's deaths (e.g., in Tharparkar, Sindh in 2014). Meanwhile, a 2022 UN study reported that among South and Southwest Asian countries, Pakistan will have the highest projected GDP loss from climate change, amounting to 9.1% annually under the worst-case climate scenario.[95] A World Bank report, also in 2022, estimated that the combined risks of extreme climate events, environmental degradation, and air pollution could reduce Pakistan's GDP by at least 18%–20% annually by 2050 (footnote 90).

Specific parts of Pakistan are also exposed to other natural hazards—the Sindh coast to cyclones, the lower Indus River basin to seawater intrusion and basin-scale changes in sediment dynamics, the northern region to GLOFs, and the region surrounding Quetta to earthquakes. Along with a consistently high score in social vulnerability because of poverty, this high exposure to natural hazards has placed the country at constantly high disaster risk levels, landing in the top 10 countries when it comes to climate risks and impacts. It placed eighth among countries most affected by extreme weather events in 2000–2019[96] and 10th of 193 countries most vulnerable to climate-related disasters in 2022.[97]

Climate Change Policy, Legal, and Institutional Framework

Although Pakistan is a minor greenhouse gas (GHG) emitter (0.9% of global GHG emissions), the country is committed to contributing to climate change mitigation by cutting its GHG emissions without compromising its energy, food, poverty reduction, and economic growth requirements. In its 2021 updated nationally determined contributions (NDCs), the country raised its emissions reduction target from 20% in 2016 to 50% of its projected 2030 GHG emissions.[98] With the National Adaptation Plan now completed, adaptation efforts will be more vigorous and systematic to address priority areas of concern, such as the agriculture–water nexus, natural capital, urban resilience, and human capital. A range of policy actions associated with urban contribution to energy, industry, transport, and agriculture-related emissions to achieve Pakistan's NDC targets have also been suggested.[99]

Recognizing the urgency to act on climate change, the Government of Pakistan prioritized the development of enabling policies, laws, and necessary institutions. Major policies and legislation now in place include the National Climate Change Policy (NCCP) (adopted 2012, updated 2021);[100] the 2014–2030 Framework for Implementation of the Climate Change Policy (2013);[101] and the Climate Change Act (2017).[102] Besides strengthening the legal foundation of the NCCP, the Climate Change Act also mandated the creation of a high-level mechanism, the Pakistan Climate Change Council, to oversee NCCP implementation.

Disaster management and risk reduction policies (2010–2013), the implementation of which has been decentralized, came even earlier. These include the National Disaster Management Ordinance, the National Disaster Management Act, the National Risk Reduction Policy, and the National Disaster Management Plan. Implementation mechanisms were likewise established, with the foremost being the national and provincial disaster management authorities.

---

[95] UN Economic and Social Commission for Asia and the Pacific (UNESCAP). 2022. *Asia-Pacific Riskscape @ 1.5°C: Subregional Pathways for Adaptation and Resilience—Asia-Pacific Disaster Report 2022 for ESCAP Subregions: Summary for Policymakers.*
[96] Germanwatch. 2021. *Global Climate Risk Index 2021.*
[97] European Commission. 2023. *INFORM Report 2023. Shared Evidence for Managing Crises and Disasters.*
[98] Government of Pakistan. 2021. Pakistan: Updated Nationally Determined Contributions 2021.
[99] N. Javed and M. Hobson. 2022. Urban Sector Inclusion in the Revised Nationally Determined Contributions of Pakistan. *ADB Briefs.* No. 210. March.
[100] Government of Pakistan. Ministry of Climate Change. 2021. *National Climate Change Policy. Updated October 2021.*
[101] Government of Pakistan, Climate Change Division. 2013. *Framework for Implementation of Climate Change Policy (2014-2030).*
[102] Senate Secretariat. 2017. Pakistan Climate Change Act, 2017. *The Gazette of Pakistan.* 3 April.

Policy development and action planning have also gained substantial headway in the provinces. Building on the environment as a devolved subject under the 18th Amendment, KP came up with its climate change policy in 2017 and updated such policy with a more detailed agenda across sectors in 2022.[103] Correspondingly, in 2021–2022, federal and/or provincial authorities collaborated with development partners and other stakeholders to develop Sindh's Climate Change Policy,[104] Punjab's Provincial Climate Change Action Plan,[105] and Stakeholder Recommendations for Climate Change Implementation, Balochistan.[106] All these policy documents have identified priority actions, and although some may still need to be formally adopted, they provide essential points for consideration in integrating climate change into urban planning and development.

In the international arena, Pakistan ratified the United Nations Framework Convention on Climate Change in 1994. It became an official partner in the global commitment to reduce GHG emissions by endorsing the 1997 Kyoto Protocol on 10 January 2005 and the Paris Agreement on 10 November 2016.[107] While raising its GHG emissions reduction target, Pakistan also highlighted the support it needs from the international community in its 2021 NDC report (footnote 98).

Climate Change and the Urban Sector

Urbanization and Climate Change

The link between urbanization and climate change is deep and multifaceted. Cities are the largest source of carbon emissions, accounting for 75% of global emissions.[108] They have the highest levels of pollution, which could aggravate temperature increases and inversions, and are the main agents of land use change. On the other hand, cities potentially face the greatest impacts from climate-related disasters as they are densely populated and have a high concentration of infrastructure, facilities, and services. The increasing densification and overcrowding in urban settlements also make cities an effective conveyor of infectious and communicable diseases, many of which are exacerbated by climate change.

Additionally, cities trigger some climate-related impacts and/or phenomena peculiar to urban settings. An example is the urban heat island (UHI) effect, which emanates from trapped heat in concrete urban surfaces and infrastructure. The UHI worsens urban air and soil quality, creates health risks to urban communities, and has become alarmingly pernicious in recent years. Another example is soil sealing, a result of thick concrete overlaid on urban spaces that leads to the loss of the soil's natural drainage capacity.

Given the above intricate and inextricable links, cities have a key role in climate change mitigation and adaptation. They must transition to low-carbon and climate-resilient development through the integration of climate change in all aspects of urban planning and management.

---

[103] Government of Khyber Pakhtunkhwa, Environmental Protection Agency. Forestry, Environment & Wildlife Department. 2022. *Khyber Pakhtunkhwa Climate Change Policy 2022*.
[104] Government of Sindh. 2021. Environment, Climate Change and Coastal Development Department. *Sindh Climate Change Policy 2022*.
[105] Government of Pakistan, Ministry of Climate Change. 2021. *Punjab Provincial Climate Change Action Plan (Draft—Suggested Actions)*.
[106] Civil Society Coalition for Climate Change; European Union; Environmental Protection Agency, Balochistan; and Ministry of Climate Change. Undated. *Stakeholder Recommendations for Climate Change Implementation Framework, Balochistan*.
[107] United Nations Climate Change. Pakistan.
[108] UN Environment Programme. Cities and Climate Change.

Urban Flooding

The increasing imperviousness of urban surfaces due to a loss of green cover and the soil sealing that comes with massive construction works and infrastructure development in cities is a major factor behind urban flooding. Lahore provides a good example. It became more prone to flooding after it lost more green cover in just 7 years (2010–2017) than it did in the previous 2 decades.[109]

Urban flooding is exacerbated by the aging and overburdened drainage systems, lack of rainwater storage and management systems, inadequate waste disposal systems, institutional capacity constraints, weak urban governance and development that ignores topography and landscape.

Urban Environment Degradation

Pakistani cities face several environmental challenges, including air, water, and land pollution. Air pollution is severe, with the levels of particulate matter and nitrous oxide in major cities higher than allowed by the National Environmental Quality Standards. Transport and industrial emissions are the biggest air pollutants. Lack of proper waste management significantly contributes to urban air, water, and soil pollution.

The social and economic costs of environmental degradation in Pakistan are significant. Air pollution alone shortens the average Pakistani's life expectancy by 4.3 years and imposes an additional loss of 6.5% of GDP per year due to mortality and years lived with disability (footnote 90).

Climate Resilience Through Adaptation and Mitigation

Climate- and Disaster-Resilient Cities

Pakistan's high exposure to climate-related hazards, such as floods, droughts, and cyclones, and its lack of coping capacity will make it continually vulnerable to climate disaster risks. Therefore, mainstreaming climate mitigation and adaptation measures in development is not an option but an imperative. With urban areas especially vulnerable and likely to bear the brunt of climate change impacts, urban focal agencies and planners need to be proactive and lose no time in adopting climate resiliency principles and approaches in development planning and management.

A necessary first step is to conduct a climate risk and vulnerability assessment, which will help identify aspects of the development plans and processes that need to be strengthened. The risk assessment is already being carried out for projects financed by development partners. Regardless of the funding source, the country's Climate Change Act, NCCP and Implementation Framework, and 18th Amendment provide the mandate and opportunity for federal and provincial agencies to institutionalize climate-proofing of all development interventions.

An ecosystem approach may be considered to ensure the climate resilience of urban development. This approach entails putting nature and the natural environment on par with other considerations in the development equation. It also means considering not just an aspect of the natural environment and ecosystem but also its intricate and dynamic interconnections with the subsystems making up the urban development landscape (i.e., physical, social, built, natural, and institutional) and aligning them individually and collectively with climate resilience objectives. Green infrastructure, nature-based solutions, and ecosystem-wide adaptation are among the latest innovations that may be explored.

---

[109] B. Iqbal. Undated. Flooded Cities: Managing Stormwater in Pakistan. CPDR. Consortium for Development Policy Research. Blog post.

The ecosystem approach will facilitate the incorporation of climate-sensitive spatial and land use planning into the master planning exercise. Green infrastructure closely integrated with gray infrastructure in town planning means more green streets, urban forestry, drainage corridors, and green open spaces such as parks and wetlands. The adoption of green technologies to adapt and complement buildings and infrastructure enhances their efficiency and ability to cope with floods, storms, and heat. It has been demonstrated in several initiatives worldwide, including some supported by the Asian Development Bank (ADB) in the Greater Mekong Subregion.[110] Lessons from these experiences informed the preparation and design of investment projects to make selected cities in the KP and Punjab provinces more livable and resilient.[111]

National Adaptation and Mitigation Initiatives

Besides strengthening the enabling environment and institutions for climate action, the government has also set in motion a wide range of adaptation and mitigation initiatives. These initiatives include Plant for Pakistan, Clean Green Pakistan, Billion Trees Tsunami Program, Protected Areas Initiatives, and Recharge Pakistan, which have increasingly gained support from key stakeholders.[112]

The plantation program in urban forests covers some of Pakistan's most populated cities: Lahore, Karachi, Multan, and Peshawar. Once established, the urban forests will contribute to both climate change adaptation and mitigation by reducing the UHI effect and through carbon sequestration. In connection with the government's Clean Green Pakistan campaign, the Pakistan Navy launched its fifth mangrove plantation campaign, planting over 3 million more mangrove seedlings in the coastal areas of Sindh and Balochistan in 2020. This brought its total planted mangroves to more than 9 million over the last 4–5 years, a unique contribution to national adaptation and mitigation efforts.[113] Meanwhile, Pakistan's national parks increased from 30 to 45, just a year after the Protected Areas Initiative was started during the COVID-19 pandemic.

Pakistan remains committed to realizing its untapped renewable energy potential—in hydro, solar, and wind—and shifting its energy mix to 60% clean energy by 2030. This clean energy transition is complemented by the implementation of the country's first electric vehicle policy in 2019, targeting 30% of vehicles to go electric by 2030.[114] Furthermore, the world's first "zero emissions" metro line project designed to utilize methane from cattle dung to power buses has been approved for Karachi.[115] Along with the implementation of the National Energy Efficiency and Conservation Act 2023, the clean energy transition will drive the attainment of Pakistan's higher emissions reduction target under its updated 2021 NDC.

Provincial governments have also started their climate actions. The Government of Punjab has incorporated into the *Punjab Spatial Strategy 2047* climate-resilient infrastructure and the greening of 10 of its large and intermediate cities (footnote 78). Under the Punjab Growth Strategy 2023, it has initiated structural and nonstructural measures to strengthen its cities' resilience to floods and droughts.

---

[110] ADB. 2016. *Nature-Based Solutions for Building Resilience in Towns and Cities: Case Studies from the Greater Mekong Subregion.*
[111] See for example: ADB. Pakistan: Khyber Pakhtunkhwa Cities Improvement Projects; and ADB. Pakistan: Developing Resilient Environments and Advancing Municipal Services in Punjab Project.
[112] Civil Society Coalition for Climate Change (CSCCC). 2018. *Role of Private Sector in Climate Action.*
[113] In addition to acting as nurseries for fish, shrimp, and other aquatic life, mangroves attenuate wave energy and storm surges, thereby protecting the coastal belt and often vulnerable people from rising sea levels. They stabilize the shorelines and are an incredible mechanism for carbon sequestration and storage. U. Ahmed. 2020. PN's Mangrove Plantation Campaign: Sustaining the Sustenance. *The News International.* 18 May.
[114] Government of Pakistan, MOCC. 2019. *National Electric Vehicle Policy.*
[115] ADB. Karachi Bus Rapid Transit Red Line Project.

Urban Needs Assessment

Housing

Urban housing has failed to keep pace with rapid urban population growth. The housing shortage estimated to have approached 10 million housing units in 2018,[116] has forced around 57% of the urban population[117] to live in slums or *katchi abadis* (informal settlements), usually under harsh and unhygienic conditions. No recent update is available on Pakistan's urban housing deficit, but the World Bank has reported a 1% decline in the proportion of the urban population living in slums from 2018 to 2020.[118]

Katchi Abadis

Katchi abadis occupy green and open spaces, rights-of-way of railroads and traffic arteries, *nullahs* (ravines), and riverbanks. They disrupt a city's functions, increase its vulnerability to flooding, and degrade its environment. Under political pressure, the provincial governments regularized *katchi abadis* in Karachi and Lahore, giving them titles or the right to abode in accordance with their respective local *katchi abadi* acts.[119] *Katchi abadi* improvement programs were initiated even before the passage of the acts; however, they had mixed results, and eventually petered out.[120] To date, less than half of the *katchi abadi* abodes in the two cities have been regularized, while they have continued to proliferate (footnote 35).

New Urban Expansions

New urban expansions provide a contrasting picture to *katchi abadis*. These new developments, which are based on the suburban single-family housing model and encroach into agricultural lands, result in car-dependent urban developments that intensify congestion and compromise the sustainability of cities. The politician–developer nexus has facilitated the rise of exclusive, gated communities that further segregate cities into rich and poor areas, potentially fueling urban tensions.[121]

---

[116] UNDP Pakistan. 2019. Urbanisation in Pakistan.
[117] A. Hasan. 2020. Karachi, informal settlements and COVID-19. Blog post. International Institute for Environment and Development (IIED).
[118] World Bank. Data. Population Living in Slums (% of Urban Population)—Pakistan (accessed 12 July 2023).
[119] Punjab Laws Online. The Punjab *Katchi Abadi* Act, 1992 (Act VIII of 1992); and Imarat Institute of Policy Studies. 2022. Sindh *Katchi Abadi* Act – Regularizing Karachi's Squatter Settlements. *Iqbal Blogs*. 21 April.
[120] Z. Nasreen and A. Hira. 2009. Impact Evaluation of *Katchi Abadis* Regularization and Development Programme (Case Study Lahore, Pakistan). Lahore: Department of City and Regional Planning, University of Engineering and Technology, Lahore. Thesis.
[121] A. Hasan and H. Arif. 2018. Pakistan: The Causes and Repercussions of the Housing Crisis. *IIED Working Paper*. IIED.

Rising Land Speculation

In the 1970s, open plot development projects for low-income groups were launched in Karachi. However, as the cost of these plots was too high for the low-income groups, people from the affluent middle class bought most of the plots.[122] This became the springboard for speculative land investment schemes that have seen the wealthier middle class acquire housing on land offered by urban development authorities. With urban development authorities virtually turning into property developers, low-income groups have been further marginalized as urban land prices continue to spiral due to increasing shortages.

The lack of access to land by low-income groups is rooted in age-old inequalities in land distribution (footnote 37). To preserve the status quo, the landed elite has worked in various ways to ensure its grip on power and deflect policies that could tilt the balance in favor of a more equitable arrangement. Efforts to address the impediments in access to land and affordable housing have thus been met with resistance from the landed elite and thwarted.

One example is the enhanced national housing policy formulated in 2001 but never formally adopted. The proposed policy included legislative and administrative measures to ensure tenure security; increase the accessibility of affordable land, finance, and housing services; and involve the private sector in housing schemes for low-income groups. Instead of adopting the policy, the government has provided ad hoc incentives to buyers, builders, developers, and commercial banks. These incentives include an array of tax exemptions on real estate and property development that, in addition to depriving the government of much-needed tax revenues, have channeled investments away from the more productive sectors of manufacturing and agribusiness into speculative land and property development ventures.[123] This has done little to increase the affordable housing supply; instead, it has facilitated the growth of the upper-income housing markets.

Government pronouncements to meet the escalating housing deficit have not translated into practice in the face of the realpolitik of the vested interests at play. For instance, government agencies that control nearly 90% of the public land in Karachi have been reluctant to release even a portion of that land for affordable housing development (footnote 84). With a monthly mortgage repayment of PRs20,000 (roughly $70 in December 2023), the Naya Pakistan Housing Program launched by the federal government in 2020 is clearly not targeting low-income groups. By mid-2023, the program had completed only 53,000 housing units (with another 28,000 under construction), well short of the target to provide 5 million housing units to those currently not owning an independent residential unit in Pakistan.[124]

As the urban population continues to swell, the country's housing shortage will be hard to address without public–private partnerships (PPPs) that target the more affordable end of the housing market (including vertical housing developments). The PPP Unit of the Government of Sindh has initiated some housing sector interventions but has yet to make an impact. As the role of the government shifts from being an executor to an enabler and facilitator of private housing development for poor people, the need to establish a legal and regulatory framework to contain the market pressure to serve the interests of nonpoor people will remain a key challenge.

---

[122] A. Hasan. 1992. *Seven Reports on Housing. Government Policies and Informal Sector and Community Responses.* Karachi: Orangi Pilot Project Research and Training Institute for the Development of *Katchi Abadis*.
[123] Invest Pakistan and Bureau of Investment. Housing and Construction. Incentives Offered by the Government.
[124] Naya Pakistan Housing and Development Authority. Housing Units—Summary (accessed 20 May 2023).

Water and Sanitation

In 2015, the World Resources Institute ranked Pakistan 23rd among 33 countries likely to experience very high water stress levels by 2040.[125] Amid rising temperatures, rapid population increase, and low water storage capacity, the country was extracting 74.3% of its freshwater resources annually. Per capita annual water availability consequently declined from 2,172 cubic meters in 1999 to 1,306 cubic meters in 2015.[126] A 2015 International Monetary Fund study[127] revealed an even bleaker situation: water availability plunged to 1,017 cubic meters per person in 2015, just 17 points away from the absolute water scarcity mark of 1,000 cubic meters per person per year.[128]

As the water crisis loomed, international and local development agencies provided critical financial and other support to avert the deterioration of water and sanitation indicators. Notwithstanding the water crisis, the proportion of the total population using safely managed water services rose, albeit incrementally, to 51% in 2022—57% in urban areas and 47% in rural areas (Figure 24).[129] The ratio of the population with access to improved sanitation,[130] including hygienically improved latrines and sewer connections, also increased.[131]

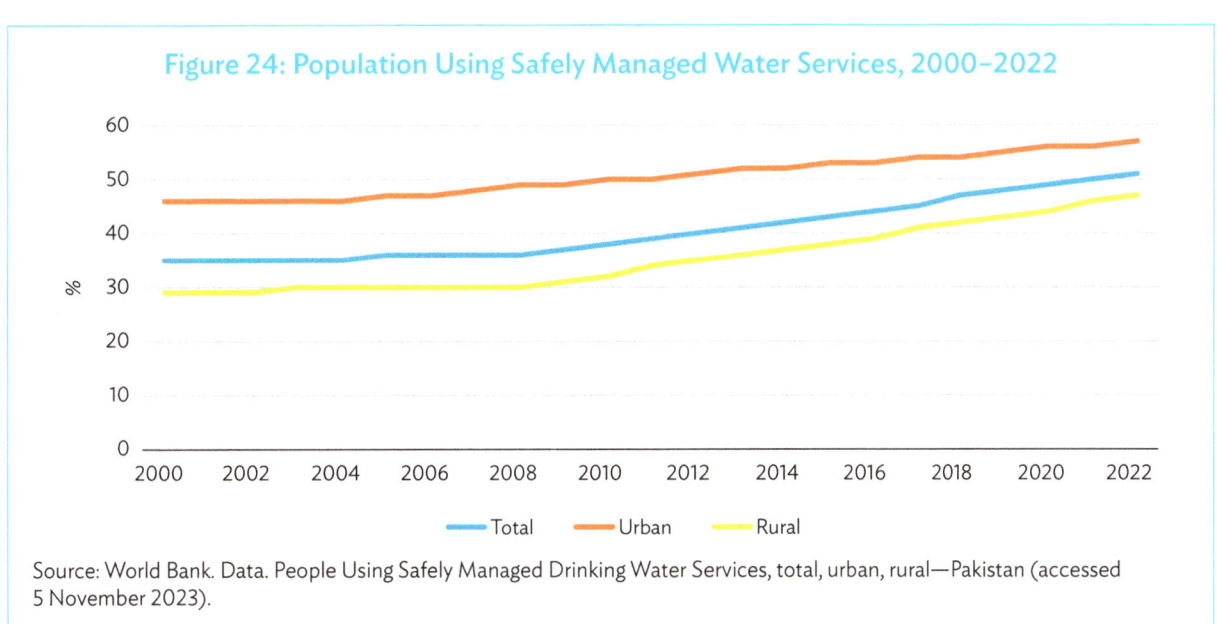

Figure 24: Population Using Safely Managed Water Services, 2000–2022

Source: World Bank. Data. People Using Safely Managed Drinking Water Services, total, urban, rural—Pakistan (accessed 5 November 2023).

---

[125] T. Luo, R.S. Young, and P. Reig. 2015. *Technical Note. Aqueduct Projected Water Stress Country Rankings*. World Resources Institute.
[126] UNDP Pakistan. 2016. Water Security in Pakistan: Issues and Challenges. *Development Advocate Pakistan*. 3 (4).
[127] International Monetary Fund. 2015. Issues in Managing Water Challenges and Policy Instruments: Regional Perspectives and Case Studies.
[128] Countries are under water stress if freshwater availability hits 1,000–1,700 cubic meters per person per year. Below this threshold, countries are under water scarcity conditions (footnote 12, p. 13).
[129] Access to safely managed water services means that drinking water from an improved source is accessible at home, available when needed, and free from fecal and priority chemical contamination.
[130] Refers to sanitation facilities that hygienically separate human waste from human contact, including flush or pour-flush to piped sewer systems, septic tank pit latrines, ventilated-improved pit latrines, or pit latrines with slab or composting toilets. They are different from basic sanitation facilities that, without necessarily avoiding human contact, enable safe disposal of human waste and maintenance of hygienic conditions through services such as garbage collection, industrial and/or hazardous waste management, and wastewater treatment and disposal.
[131] World Health Organization (WHO)/United Nations Children's Fund (UNICEF) Joint Programme for Monitoring Water Supply, Sanitation and Hygiene, eds. 2023. *Progress on Household Drinking-Water, Sanitation and Hygiene 2000–2022: Special Focus on Gender*. UNICEF and WHO.

Despite the improvements, huge deficits remain, even in urban areas. As of 2022, some 39 million or 43% of Pakistani urban dwellers did not have access to a safely managed water service, while an estimated 15.7 million or 18% of urban dwellers lacked access to a basic sanitation service. Underpinning the deficits is a web of interlinked issues. District-level data from the Pakistan Social and Living Standards Measurement Survey 2019–2020 provide a glimpse of the nature and extent of the deficits in the country's major cities (Table 8).

Table 8: Urban Population in Major Cities with Access to Water and Sanitation, 2020
(% of Households)

City or District	Source of Drinking Water				Toilet		
	Tap Water (↓ or ↑ from 2015)	Non-Tap Water			Flush (↓ or ↑ from 2015)	Non-Flush	No Toilet
		Filtration Pump	Mobile (Truck or Tanker)	Others (Pumps, Wells, etc.)			
Karachi Central	68.88 (↓15)	1.87	1.74	27.1	98[a]	1	...
Karachi East	62.62[a]	4.01	1.65	31.72	100[a]	0	0
Karachi Malir[b]	85.03[a]	6.98	0.96	7.03	100[a]	0	0
Karachi South	69.91[a]	2.49	2.34	25.26	100[a]	0	0
Karachi West[b]	57.28[a]	2.73	27.18	12.81	99[a]	1	0
Korangi	70.70[a]	0.57	5.51	23.22	100 (↑57)	0	0
Hyderabad[b]	78.12 (↑17)	3.42	0.22	18.24	95 (↑12)	3	2
Lahore	23.29 (↓36)	57.27	0.38	19.06	99 (↔)	...	...
Faisalabad[b]	12.81 (↓0.2)	27.3	40.49	19.4	100 (↑8)	0	0
Gujranwala[b]	6.54 (↑1.5)	37.28	15	41.18	100 (↑6)	0	0
Rawalpindi[b]	32.41 (↑0.4)	21.18	0.34	46.07	99 (↑5)	0	1
Multan[b]	18.29 (↑8)	21.66	0.47	59.58	99 (↑24)	0	1
Bahawalpur[b]	15.17 (↓1.2)	16.75	1.10	66.98	99 (↑29)	0	1
Sargodha[b]	11.06 (↑5)	0.68	0.94	87.32	98 (↑20)	0	2
Sialkot[b]	16.65 (↓2.4)	58.66	0.39	24.3	100 (↑5)	0	0
Peshawar[b]	73.28 (↑24)	0.11	0.00	26.61	99 (↑11)	...	...
Quetta	42.41 (↑28)	0.59	45.06	11.94	89 (↑13)	11	1
Islamabad[b]	24.37 (↑4)	19.4	2.43	53.8	99 (↔)	0	1

↑ = increase, ↓ = decrease, ↔ = no change, ... = no data.

Notes:
1. Urban and rural areas in Pakistan, delineated by provincial governments and/or cantonment boards, represent administrative boundaries; therefore, it is not unusual for a city or district to have both urban and rural areas.
2. Ellipses indicate possible lack of data in cases where the available statistics, representing percentages, do not sum up to 100%.
3. Directional arrows, also representing percentages, reflect upward and downward movements or no change from previous data referenced in the survey report.

[a] No data in 2015.
[b] With both urban and rural areas.

Source: Pakistan Bureau of Statistics. 2021. *PSLM 2019–20 Pakistan Social and Living Standards Measurement Survey (2019–20)*. District Level. Table 7.1 and Table 7.2.

Water Supply in Key Cities

Availability, adequacy, and accessibility. While steps have been taken to augment existing sources, water supply in the country's key cities has largely been irregular, inequitable, and unable to meet demand. According to a WWF study, water in Karachi is provided for only 2 hours every 2 days, or at best, 2–4 hours every day.[132] Water started to be rationed in Lahore and other cities in Punjab in 2018, available intermittently from the pipes for only about 12 hours a day, if at all.[133] Similarly, in 2017, all cities in KP had access to tap water, typically for only 6 hours or less per day.[134] Quetta's inability to meet even a third of its daily water needs has already affected citizens' quality of life and without action, large parts of the population might be forced to migrate.

Besides being irregular and unreliable, water supply networks have also been unable to fully cover their intended service areas. As of 2019, the Karachi Water and Sanitation Board (KWSB) reached only 55% of the city's population (footnote 132). Though relatively higher, the Water and Sanitation Agency (WASA), Lahore served just 61.6% of the population of the city in 2022.[135] In KP, the water and sanitation services companies (WSSCs), operating as corporatized public utilities alongside city development authorities, covered only 48% the urban population in 2017 (footnote 134).

The unserved groups in all major cities are primarily poor people in overcrowded communities and those living on city peripheries. These inequalities in access are confirmed by UNICEF and WHO Joint Monitoring Programme data, which indicate that in 2018, the wealthiest 20% of the population had 1.2 times the access to a basic water service and 3.3 times the access to a basic sanitation service as compared to the poorest 20% of the population (footnote 131).

Underlying constraints. Localized depletion of water sources, both ground and surface, is a major factor behind the worsening water supply shortages in Pakistan. This converges with aging and inadequate infrastructure, a lack of proper maintenance, underinvestment, and weak institutions and governance to further constrain the ability of the cities and their water supply networks to meet the needs of their growing populations.

In Karachi, the Karachi Water and Sewerage Corporation (KWSC) has never fully met the city's long-standing 820–1,200 million gallons per day (mgd) water supply requirement (footnote 132). In 2019, KWSC typically produced only 655 mgd of water, drawn solely from nearby lakes due to the high salinity levels of Karachi's groundwater. With water losses of 35%–58% of the water generated due to physical leakages and rampant water theft, the utility only supplies 433 mgd or 36%–53% of Karachi's water demand.

With only 25% of industrial and commercial customers metered, zero metering of retail customers, very low water tariffs (averaging $0.13 per cubic meter), and tariff collection below 50%, the KSWC has never come close to achieving cost-recovery.[136] As such, it depends mainly on provincial allocations, which are influenced by partisan politics, for its O&M needs. In practice, this has meant inadequate funding for routine maintenance over extended periods. Without essential changes in KWSC management, operational policies, and the overall institutional framework, the political economy of water services in Karachi could remain problematic.

---

[132] WWF-Pakistan. 2019. Situational Analysis of Water Resources of Karachi. *Issue Brief*.
[133] W. Mustafa. 2018. *As Groundwater Levels Plunge, Lahore Begins Turning Off Taps*. Reuters. 10 October.
[134] ADB. 2018. Khyber Pakhtunkhwa Cities Improvement Project. Sector Assessment (Summary): Water and Other Urban Infrastructure and Services. In *Report and Recommendation of the President to the Board of Directors. Islamic Republic of Pakistan. Khyber Pakhtunkhwa Cities Improvement Project*.
[135] M. Abbas, S. Kazama, and S. Takizawa. 2022. Water Demand Estimation in Service Areas with Limited Numbers of Customer Meters—Case Study in Water and Sanitation Agency (WASA) Lahore, Pakistan. *Water*. 14 (14). pp. 2197.
[136] W.J. Young et al. 2019. *Pakistan. Getting More from Water*. World Bank Group.

In Lahore and Quetta, as in most other groundwater-dependent cities in Punjab and Balochistan, localized groundwater depletion has become a major concern. Lahore's water table has been receding alarmingly at about 1 meter per year, exacerbated by the fact that only 297 mgd of the 540 mgd water produced by the city's WASA reaches its customers due to 45% nonrevenue water loss.[137] The higher electricity costs required to extract water from deeper underground sources further constrains water supply, particularly in the many small and intermediate cities in Punjab. This is particularly pronounced in Quetta, where tube wells must be at least 244–305 meters deep just to reach the groundwater table.

Across KP urban areas, leakage in piped water distribution exceeds 50%, exacerbating the constraints posed by inadequate storage capacity, unreliable power supplies, and dwindling groundwater resources on urban water supply in the province (footnote 134). All the cities are dependent on groundwater as their source of water, except for Peshawar and Abbottabad, which draw 10% of their supplies from surface water.

Islamabad depends on both surface and groundwater sources for its water supplies but faces water-sharing issues with the provinces. Consequently, production capacity is limited to 84 mgd as compared to the average estimated demand of 176 mgd (footnote 35). Leaking and rusted distribution pipes combine with inefficient and obsolete distribution technologies to negatively impact the reliability of access to water and its safety.

While access to safe drinking water of the urban population improved from 2015 to 2022, the use of piped water as the primary source of drinking water decreased from 49% to 39% (footnote 131). The *2019–2020 Pakistan Social and Living Standards Measurement (PSLM) Survey* results indicate the source of improvement as the increased use of filtration plants, which rose from 6% of the total urban households in 2015 to 19% in 2020 (footnote 8).

Water theft and related issues. Water theft in Karachi was valued in 2017 at over $500 million a year (footnote 136). Several studies have found water theft occurring at various points in the supply chain and this persists until today.[138] The phenomenon reflects deep-seated problems with water laws and policies and weak enforcement. Eliminating theft is essential for local and provincial governments to address the multifaceted elements of the water crises facing Pakistan's cities. Managing water theft requires robust technical and financial systems—including network rehabilitation, universal retail and bulk water supply connections and metering, reducing nonrevenue water, and implementing a tariff system that at least aims for cost-recovery and adequate O&M.

Water quality. Surface and groundwater sources are routinely contaminated with coliform, toxic metals, pesticides, and even contaminants from the pharmaceutical industry.[139] This contamination has contributed to the high incidence of diarrhea among Pakistani children, the 23rd highest worldwide. As of 2017, diseases such as cholera, typhoid, dysentery, hepatitis, and guinea worm infections from contaminated drinking water and poor sanitation comprised 80% of all illnesses and accounted for 33% of deaths.[140]

The situation improved following a campaign to eliminate the practice of open defecation, which intensified under the Pakistan Approach to Total Sanitation, a strategy to scale up sanitation programs developed and implemented by the Government of Pakistan in the aftermath of the 2010 floods. UN reports indicate that open defecation has been practically abolished in urban areas, although it continues to be practiced by 12% of the

---

[137] Asian Infrastructure Investment Bank. 2018. Project Summary Information (PSI). Lahore Water and Wastewater Management Project.
[138] J. Khurshid. 2023. SHC [Sindh High Court] Directs KWSB to Take Action Against Illegal Hydrants in District West. *The News International*. 10 April.
[139] M. Fida et al. 2022. Water Contamination and Human Health Risks in Pakistan: A Review. *Exposure and Health*. 15 (3). pp. 1–21.
[140] M.K. Daud et al. 2017. Drinking Water Quality Status and Contamination in Pakistan. *Biomed Research International*. 7908183.

rural population.[141] This helped reduce the incidence of diarrhea among children across Pakistan's provinces, except in Sindh, from 2015 to 2020 (footnote 8). The country still has a long way to go to reduce contamination from industrial and agriculture waste that circles back to the cities and endangers human health through the food chain.

Sanitation

While 97% of Pakistan's urban households have sanitary toilets as of 2020 (Table 8), not all of them have access to a proper sewage disposal system (Figure 25). Significant amounts of the country's wastewater, mostly untreated, continue to be discharged into open drains, streams, rivers, and other water bodies, damaging aquatic and marine ecosystems and contaminating both surface water and groundwater.

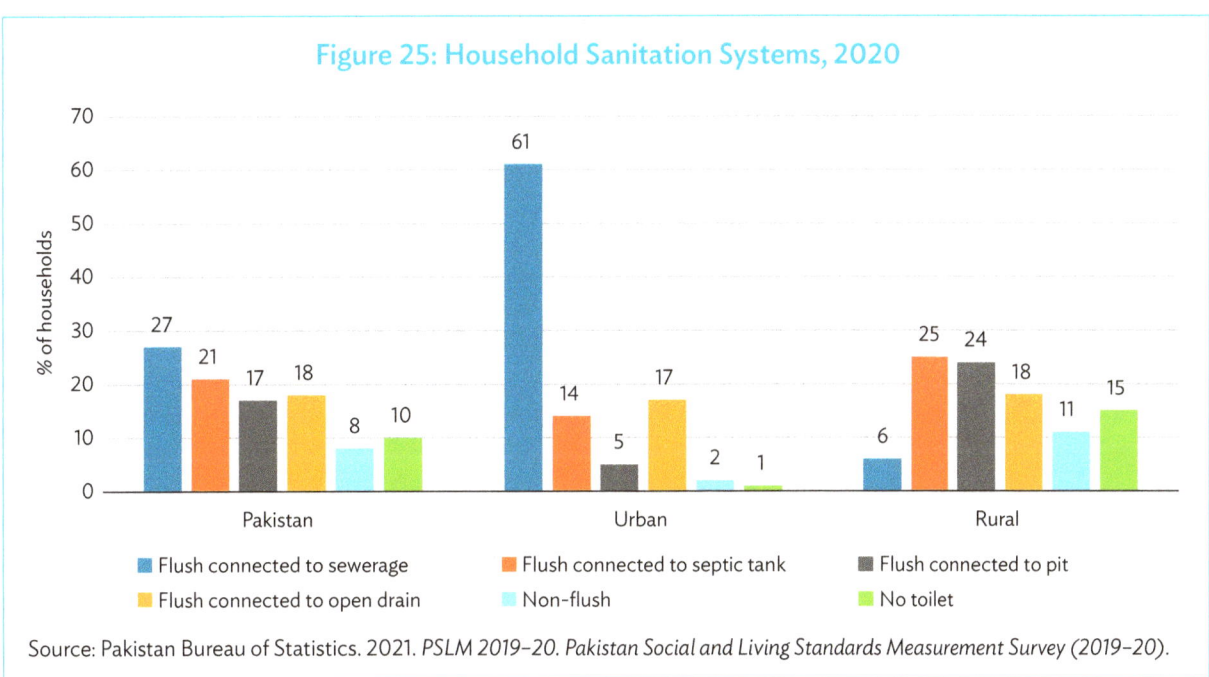

Figure 25: Household Sanitation Systems, 2020

Source: Pakistan Bureau of Statistics. 2021. *PSLM 2019–20. Pakistan Social and Living Standards Measurement Survey (2019–20)*.

Wastewater management. In all cities of Punjab, inadequate sewerage infrastructure is a serious problem. The province has only two wastewater treatment plants (WWTPs), with capacities below requirements. The bigger WWTP in Faisalabad can handle only 30% of the city's wastewater, while the smaller one in Multan can handle much less. Lahore currently has no WWTP. While four WWTPs are under construction, six plants will be required to treat the 640 mgd of untreated domestic and industrial wastewater discharged into the Ravi River.

In KP, separate sewerage systems cover less than 5% of urban areas. These systems are poorly maintained and particularly prone to rainwater ingress causing periodic overflows (footnote 134). In most urban areas, sewage combined with rainwater is conveyed by open drains onto farmlands for use in irrigation. In addition to degrading the environment, the practice poses a serious health hazard to local farmers and adjacent communities and puts at risk the safety of local farm produce.

---

[141] UN, UN Water, UNICEF, and WHO. 2022. *SDG 6 Country Acceleration Case Studies 2022. Pakistan.*

Although Islamabad and Karachi have WWTPs, their capacity is less than 8% of each city's industrial and municipal waste.[142] The operation of the WWTP in Islamabad is hampered by sedimentation and clogging in the sewerage network draining into it. Only two of Karachi's three major WWTPs are operational at half capacity,[143] while less than 4% of industrial units generating wastewater have WWTPs (Table 9). The huge amount of untreated industrial and municipal sewage, reaching 420 mgd in 2019, flows to the Arabian Sea through two rivers in Lyari and Maril (footnote 132).

Table 9: Wastewater Treatment Plants in Karachi's Industrial Sector, 2019

Item	Korangi	Karachi West	Karachi Malir	Karachi Central
Number of industrial units	673	1998	842	206
Industrial units generating wastewater	244	944	293	95
Industrial units with wastewater treatment plants	24	18	17	3

Source: WWF-Pakistan. 2019. Situational Analysis of Water Resources of Karachi. *Issue Brief*.

In early 2022, the federal and city governments finalized a plan to construct five combined effluent treatment plants. One of these plants, intended to treat wastewater from tanneries and sewage from one of KWSC's pumping stations, has been installed but has yet to operate at full capacity. A project to rehabilitate and operate the city's idle WWTP capacity through a PPP is currently being developed. Once fully operational, the three WWTPs will be able to handle Karachi's industrial and municipal waste.

Wastewater reuse. Wastewater treated for reuse is increasingly augmenting water and renewable energy supplies.[144] Beyond knowledge exchange and exploratory talks, strengthening the water and sanitation regulatory framework is a prerequisite for any future action on sewage disposal and wastewater treatment and reuse. The need to routinely assess and audit the performance of the existing sewerage systems is essential to garner donor and private sector interest in financing wastewater treatment and potential reuse.

Energy Supply and Demand

Current Crisis

Pakistan has historically struggled to meet its energy needs. Following significant improvements in generation capacity and despite some load shedding as distribution companies sought to reduce their losses from electricity theft and unpaid bills, most big cities did not encounter major electricity interruptions from 2016 to 2019.[145] However, the situation has changed remarkably since 2021. Massive blackouts and power outages have again hit the country. Power generation has been tremendously constrained by soaring imported fuel prices, while distribution and transmission capacity has plunged with the lack of investment in infrastructure upgrades and funds for routine maintenance and the repair of massive damage wrought by recent disasters.

---

[142] G. Murtaza and M.H. Zia 2012. Wastewater Production, Treatment and Use in Pakistan. *Country Report 2012*. UN Water.
[143] H. Khan. 2022. Karachi's Dirty Water Flows to the Ocean, Untreated. *News*. 28 June.
[144] M. Batool and L. Shahzad. 2021. An Analytical Study on Municipal Wastewater to Energy Generation, Current Trends, and Future Prospects in South Asian Developing Countries (an Update on Pakistan Scenario). *Environmental Science and Pollution Research*. 28 (7-9).
[145] Government of Pakistan. Finance Division. 2019. *Pakistan Economic Survey 2018-19*.

The country's power companies are in poor health, with circular debt and inadequate tariffs among the key causes.[146] The Finance Division acknowledges circular debt as a problem (footnote 44). It has calculated this debt at 3.8% of Pakistan's GDP and 5.6% of government debt as of March 2022. If left unaddressed, it could balloon to PRs4 trillion by FY2025, with further crippling effects on the power sector, economy, and household activities.

Renewable Energy

In FY2022, Pakistan's electricity generation comprised 60.7% thermal, 23.2% hydroelectric, 11.9% nuclear, 4.2% renewable (solar and wind), and 1% other sources.[147] Its 2020 renewable energy policy sets an ambitious target for solar and wind to reach a 30% share of the country's energy mix by 2030.

The German development agency GIZ is assisting the government in achieving that target and supporting distribution companies in integrating renewable energy, advancing distributed generation, and developing business models for off-grid energy production. It recently supported the introduction of feed-in tariffs that facilitated more renewable energy investments, net metering, and decentralized solar energy generation.

Energy Efficiency and Conservation

The National Energy Efficiency and Conservation Act (2016) aims to achieve energy savings of 9 million tons of oil equivalent by 2030. These savings will reduce carbon emissions by 35 million tons and save the national coffers $6.4 billion per year post-2030.

To execute the law, the Ministry of Energy created two federal agencies, the Pakistan Energy Efficiency and Conservation Board and the National Energy Efficiency and Conservation Authority. A strategic plan for 2020–2025 and some policies have been put in place, but progress has been sluggish. For example, the minimum energy performance standards and building energy efficiency codes have yet to gain traction.

Sector Institutions

Energy remains mainly a federal government responsibility in Pakistan despite the 18th Amendment. The devolution of distribution companies to the provinces has been considered, but provincial governments have been reluctant to accept the responsibility.

Several power generation companies, both public and private, operate in the country. There are two transmission companies, the public Pakistan-wide National Transmission & Despatch Company and the privatized K-Electric for the Karachi district, which is also involved in power generation. Ten public distribution companies (DISCOs) operate in rural and urban areas and have similar organizational and technical structures. The National Electric Power Regulatory Authority, the country's energy regulator, is entirely independent and efficient in reporting faults in the system. But as good performance is not rewarded nor underperformance penalized, publicly owned DISCOs have no motivation to improve their services.

---

[146] Circular debt occurs when an entity with cash inflow problems defers payments to its suppliers and creditors, thus causing these problems to cascade to other segments of its payment chain. In Pakistan's power sector, this shows up in the inability of the Central Power Purchasing Agency to timely meet its payment obligations to other power companies in the supply chain, including the state-owned generation companies, independent power producers, and National Transmission and Despatch Company, because of lack of timely payments from distribution companies. For more details, see: (i) S.S. Ali and S. Badar. 2010. Dynamics of Circular Debt in Pakistan and Its Resolution. *The Lahore Journal of Economics* 15: SE (September 2010). pp. 61–74, and (ii) A. Malik. 2020. Circular Debt—An Unfortunate Misnomer. *PIDE Working Paper*. No. 2020:20. Pakistan Institute of Development Economics (PIDE).

[147] National Electric Power Regulatory Authority. *State of Industry Report 2022*.

Tariffs

Pakistan's inadequate tariff regime is a complex issue undermining the DISCOs' financial sustainability. It particularly besets DISCO operations in rural areas, where 50%–70% of the serviced populations do not pay their bills, partly because of an inability to pay but also due to inefficiencies and rampant irregularities in billing and collection. By issuing stay orders delaying legal procedures for a year and allowing offenders of meter tampering and related ordinances to merely pay a fixed fine, courts contribute to the problem.

Only the privatized K-Electric is financially sustainable. The company used to suffer significant losses but recovered after privatization and has since operated from its revenue collections. Despite considerable resistance, it has succeeded in metering its expansive 6,500 km² service area, which goes beyond Karachi to five districts in Sindh and Balochistan, reducing electricity theft and a corresponding loss in income. Through load shedding, it has controlled losses from illegal connections that still exist in some areas.

Notwithstanding the successful model presented by K-Electric, political issues and strong resistance from trade unions have blocked the privatization of other DISCOs. In response, the government is considering segmentizing utility operations and infrastructure expansion, e.g., between urban and rural areas, to reduce costs and control losses. The potential of publicly offering the companies on the stock market, with the government keeping most of the shares, is also being studied.

Demand and Supply in Major Cities

There are variations in the quality of service provided in major cities. Islamabad has a continuous supply of electricity without interruptions. Shortages occur in Lahore and Karachi, mostly during summer when demand is high, though in areas where consumers pay their bills and illegal connections have been eliminated, K-Electric has provided better quality service than in the past.

Peshawar has a sufficient energy supply. Like Karachi, it has an uninterrupted supply in the city's central areas, where 90%–95% of the population are paying customers. Power disruptions occur only during severe weather due to a non-resilient distribution system.

Balochistan faces the most significant difficulties in energy supply among the provinces. Quetta accessed only 20 hours of electricity daily in 2020, while supply was lower in the city's outskirts, at 16–18 hours per day. The province's divisional and district headquarters had electricity for 12–14 hours per day, but the villages only 4–6 hours. Increased demand, significant distribution and transmission losses, bill delinquencies, and electricity theft are the main reasons for the shortages.

Solid Waste Management

Overall Situation

Solid waste generation in Pakistan ranges from 0.283 to 0.612 kilograms per capita per day and increases by 2.4% annually.[148] Despite progress, solid waste management (SWM) remains inefficient and limited, resulting in the accumulation of waste alongside roads and other open spaces. Much of this is usually burned, becoming a source of pollution and health hazard. When collected, the waste ends up in uncontrolled and unsanitary landfills

---

[148] Government of the Punjab. Environment Protection Department. Solid Waste.

or rivers, threatening aquatic life and contaminating groundwater sources. Sanitary landfills are rare, although some initiatives are taking off. In most cities, segregation of waste streams is not carried out. No formal recycling policy is in place, and scavengers picking up what they consider valuable is the only form of recycling undertaken. No waste reduction program at source has been initiated, nor are there clear citywide SWM strategies. Citizens also lack awareness of waste and environmental and public health issues.

In 2013–2014, 76% of the population reported no access to a garbage collection system; this fell only marginally to 75% in 2018–2019,[149] then 67% in 2019–2020 (footnote 8). With municipal services coverage declining sharply to 17% in 2019–2020, from 49% in 2018–2019 (Figure 26), the recent improvement is possibly due to a significant increase in private and other nongovernment-led services. In 2019–2020, municipal collection covered 39% of urban households and 2% of households in rural areas. At the provincial-level, municipal services in Sindh had the highest coverage, at 22% of its total population, with KP the lowest at 5%.

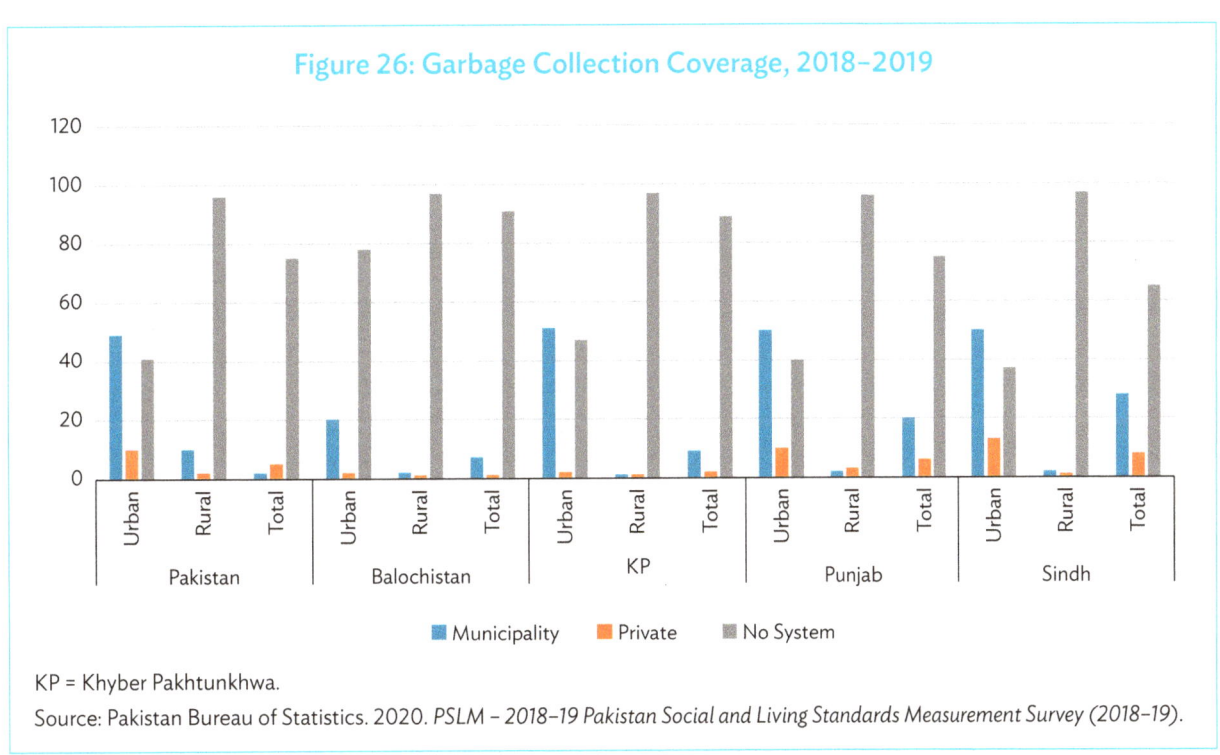

Figure 26: Garbage Collection Coverage, 2018–2019

KP = Khyber Pakhtunkhwa.
Source: Pakistan Bureau of Statistics. 2020. *PSLM – 2018-19 Pakistan Social and Living Standards Measurement Survey (2018-19)*.

Solid Waste Management in Key Cities

Lahore. The Government of Punjab established the Lahore Waste Management Company (LWMC) in 2010 to improve waste collection. Since then, eight more waste management companies have been established. Municipal corporation sanitary workers provide waste management services in the smaller cities.

The LWMC has jurisdiction over Lahore, except for cantonments and areas under the administration of private housing societies. In 2011, it deployed mechanical sweepers and washing to a broad swathe of areas, which made the city center significantly cleaner. Collection coverage was 30% door-by-door and 70% container-based.

---

[149] Pakistan Bureau of Statistics. 2020. *PSLM – 2018-19 Pakistan Social and Living Standards Measurement Survey (2018-19)*.

The LWMC outsourced waste collection to two Turkish companies until December 2020, when it switched to local contractors to reduce costs. However, as it took time for the LWMC to find suitable replacements, sanitation deteriorated before it began to improve in late 2021.

Lahore has one landfill site managed by the LWMC. The landfill has six lots, two of them for sanitary disposal of waste. However, as all six lots have reached capacity, currently, waste is openly dumped in the other four lots. The city produces 5,500–6,000 tons of garbage daily—1,000 tons go to a private refuse-derived fuel facility, 200 tons go to a compost plant near the landfill site, and 4,000 tons are disposed of at the landfill. There is no recycling or segregation at source.

The LWMC, like all other government-run waste management companies in Punjab and across Pakistan, is not financially sustainable and subsidized—the nominal sanitation fee collected comprises just 10% of LWMC's total revenues.

But things are improving. The provincial government has prepared business plans to make SWM services self-sustainable for each local government. The business plan for Lahore and the LWMC includes (i) broadening the sanitation fee collection base and increasing fines for polluters, (ii) streamlining revenue generation from refuse-derived fuel facilities and compost plants, and (iii) establishing and collecting revenue from waste-to-energy and biogas plants. Negotiations have begun to establish these projects under a PPP model.

Karachi. Before the Sindh Solid Waste Management Board (SSWMB) was established in 2014, the responsibility for waste collection in Karachi was with the Karachi Municipal Corporation. Post-2014, the SSWMB took charge of SWM in three of the city's six districts, improving SWM in them noticeably. Still, SWM in Sindh province, including Karachi, faces serious challenges. Pollution is a significant threat. Municipal waste continues to be dumped in open sites, and as it rots, it causes air, soil, and water pollution. Uncollected waste eventually finds its way to the Arabian Sea, polluting and degrading its marine and surrounding ecosystems. Garbage in Karachi is disposed of in mangroves to assist informal land reclamation and the expansion of informal settlements. No management scheme for industrial or other hazardous waste is in place. All these, combined with untreated wastewater, have completely degraded Karachi's harbor.

Peshawar. SWM in KP significantly improved after water and sanitation services companies (WSSCs) were operationalized in the province's seven cities (divisional headquarters) in 2014. The WSSCs are public limited companies owned by the Government of KP, and with a mandate to provide water and SWM services, they have systematized citywide cleaning and garbage collection. The provincial government has also initiated sewerage and SWM master plan activities.

The Water and Sanitation Services Peshawar is responsible for SWM in the capital city. Over the last 6 years, Peshawar augmented its SWM equipment and human resources, enabling it to perform better than other cities. Up to 80% of the city's 850 tons of solid waste generated daily is collected. After collection, waste is brought to an informal transfer station and then to an open landfill outside the city. Under an ADB-supported project readiness financing facility, a feasibility study on a sanitary landfill and ancillary recycling, materials recovery, waste-to-energy, and composting facilities has been prepared.

Islamabad. Islamabad used to be one of the country's cleanest cities. However, standards deteriorated due to the inadequate capacity and experience of the Municipal Corporation of Islamabad which took over SWM and other services from the Capital Development Authority (CDA) in 2015. The municipal corporation was run by the city's first elected mayor. After the service mandate was returned to the CDA by the federal government in 2020, the city's waste collection service improved again.

Islamabad's experience in SWM and other service delivery provides an example of how Pakistan's complex urban governance matrix—with overlapping roles, political interference, and institutional rivalries—obstructs the empowerment of cities and leads to poor services. Since its establishment, Islamabad has had no permanent landfill site, and authorities keep switching to temporary dumping sites. Residents and nearby communities have resisted efforts to build on a permanent place due to possible negative health impacts. However, a suitable location has recently been identified, and there is optimism the project will move forward.

Quetta. The Metropolitan Corporation Quetta has limited capacity and resources to collect and properly dispose of municipal waste. Only about one-third of the generated waste is collected from the streets. The situation is even worse in other cities of Balochistan, where SWM systems barely exist.

Urban Transport

National Backdrop

A well-functioning transportation system starts with a comprehensive master plan, adequate infrastructure provisions, and effective physical and town planning. However, these crucial components are lacking in many Pakistani cities, particularly the smaller ones, making it difficult to undertake effective transport planning. Larger cities, such as Karachi, have established their own public transport systems, albeit mainly in the informal sector. They often operate with limited oversight, standards, and infrastructure support, leading to issues such as congestion, pollution, and safety concerns.

The continuing insufficiency and limited coverage of urban public transport systems presents a significant challenge, given the rapid increase in population and the continued expansion of car-dependent suburbs. While Pakistan still has a low vehicle ownership rate, ranking 167th globally with only 30 vehicles per 1,000 people in 2022, the large cities are already clogged and this could worsen as car ownership increases.[150]

In response, the Planning Commission issued the 2018 National Transport Policy of Pakistan, providing policy directions for the various transport subsectors.[151] The policy underscored the need to develop urban transport as a single, integrated, and multimodal network that utilizes both motorized and nonmotorized transport systems. It called for the preparation of individual long-term urban transport master plans for all major cities following transit-oriented design principles and incorporating walking and cycling networks as an integral part of the urban streetscape. It also pressed for the establishment of urban transport authorities to plan and regulate local transport services, license urban public transport, develop electric and other low-carbon transport systems, and phase out internal combustion engines over time.

Issues Across Cities

The prevailing redundant urban governance model is also evident in the transport sector. Several departments and agencies are involved in road network planning, construction and maintenance supervision, and policy and regulatory support. Most cities do not have a traffic management agency; the function is shared by provincial and urban transport departments or the development authorities. In many cases, different entities manage different parts of the city with little coordination.

---

[150] CEIC Data. Number of Registered Vehicles by Country Comparison (accessed 18 September 2023).
[151] Government of Pakistan, Ministry of Planning, Development and Reform. Planning Commission. Undated. *National Transport Policy of Pakistan 2018.*

Congestion is a significant issue for all cities. Transportation is dependent on motorized vehicles that cause bottlenecks and aggravate air pollution. Traffic accidents are widespread due to aggressive driving and lack of respect for road safety rules. Individually owned small vehicles like rickshaws overwhelm the streets and intensify the chaotic urban traffic. Environment-friendly transport modes are lacking. There is no cycling culture nor appropriate infrastructure to support pedestrianization. Lack of gender responsiveness and inclusivity is also an issue: women often face harassment and misconduct while using urban transport networks, restricting their mobility, social interaction, and opportunities for self-agency and development.

City-Level Challenges

Recently completed mass transit systems have improved transport in cities like Peshawar and Lahore. However, they are considered by some stakeholders as expensive for the government, so a life-cycle analysis to evaluate their cost-effectiveness may be necessary. The provision of mass transit systems, however, is still not enough to address the severe transport problems of major cities. The need for a holistic approach, which combines improvements in land use and zoning, multiple modes of transport, and the integration of public transport network development and management, especially at the metropolitan level, should be emphasized.

Across Punjab. In 2012, the Government of Punjab established the Punjab Masstransit Authority (PMA) to promote public mass transportation in the province. The PMA operates in the cities of Lahore, Rawalpindi, Multan, and Faisalabad. Lahore, Rawalpindi, and Multan have bus rapid transit (BRT) systems, while Lahore and Multan have bus feeder systems through a PPP arrangement.

According to the PMA, a 20%–25% commuter shift to BRT followed the operation of the first metro bus in Lahore. In contrast, the BRT line in Multan has suffered from low passengers, with people continuing to use motorcycles and rickshaws. While they should have been a city responsibility, mass transit systems remain under provincial supervision. There is no central metropolitan transport authority with adequate capacity to handle this responsibility in any of the four cities under the jurisdiction of the PMA.

Lahore. The number of registered vehicles in Lahore has doubled in the last decade (footnote 35). The city has constructed numerous underpasses to ease congestion and completed a large part of the Lahore Ring Road, an 85-kilometer highway that encircles the city. Despite this, Lahore still suffers from congestion and an inadequate public transport system. Essential steps have been taken in recent years to improve the public transport network, with the inauguration of a BRT line in 2013 and the first metro line for the whole country, the Orange Line, in late 2020.

The Orange Line is expected to significantly improve the city's traffic conditions, with half a million passengers projected to use the service daily by 2025. However, the original plan to regenerate the areas around each station with mixed-use, high-rise development has not yet materialized.

PMA's long-term plans include two more metro lines and the completion of eight phases of feeder routes. It already runs a bus feeder route system for the Green Line, while the Lahore Transport Company oversees the bus network for the rest of the city. However, the transport company faces significant operational issues, leading to low-quality service and disruptions.

Karachi. The city experiences severe congestion worsening by the day. Private car and motorbike usage is increasing and pollution is rising, although efforts are made to test vehicles regularly to reduce emissions. Vertical expansion is progressing; however, without integrating mixed-use, specifically the establishment of commercial and recreational spaces alongside the construction of high-rise new residential buildings, this could only aggravate the traffic problem. The scenario is likely to be reinforced by a requirement for developers to provide 1.5 parking spaces for every dwelling unit in all new residential buildings.

The federal government aims to revive the city's circular railway and is planning several BRT lines. The Green BRT Line funded by the federal government started operations in 2021, while the Orange BRT Line funded by the province started in 2022. The Yellow and Red lines, financed by ADB and the World Bank, are in their construction phase. The plan for a Blue Line—the fifth BRT line—was abandoned after the private investor, the Bahria Town Group, withdrew from the project. The line, which intended to connect Karachi with the company's private development northeast of the city, would have been the first privately funded BRT line in the country.

The entire institutional and legal framework for Karachi's future mass transit systems was developed through an ADB-supported initiative. ADB assisted the provincial government in establishing the regulator, the Sindh Mass Transit Authority, and the operator, the TransKarachi Company. A mass transit network will ease the mobility and congestion problems in the city, but it will need constant upgrading considering the rapid population growth and increasing dependence on cars in the new urban expansions. As with all major cities, a holistic, sustainable public transport plan is imperative.

Peshawar. Public transport in Peshawar has improved recently compared with other big cities. The newly constructed BRT line managed by the Government of KP's Transport Department has already brought positive impacts. The ADB-funded project was inaugurated in August 2020 and became popular despite COVID-19 mobility restrictions. In Mardan and Abbottabad, the UN Office for Project Services, with funding from the Government of Japan, initiated a women-only bus service nicknamed "The Pink Bus Service" in 2018.[152] The initiative, as with a similar earlier project in Lahore,[153] aims to support women in overcoming mobility constraints and empower them to participate in political, social, and economic life.[154]

Islamabad. In 2014, the CDA completed a mass transit system study identifying six priority routes. Two BRT routes, between Rawalpindi and Islamabad and Islamabad to the new international airport, are now operational. The PMA operates the existing BRT lines with a federal government subsidy. Currently, the CDA is responsible for transport planning in Islamabad, while Rawalpindi has its transport authority. The transport problems faced by the two cities are interconnected. Rather than having two administrative structures working in parallel, a single authority overseeing public transport network development in both cities may be a better approach.

Quetta. Neither Quetta nor any other city in Balochistan has any public transport system. Quetta endures severe traffic congestion. The city's commercial activity, which caters to the entire region's needs, is concentrated in a 2-km radius from its center, usually bottlenecked. Multiple, dispersed commercial centers would ease the situation.

---

[152] M. Ahil. 2018. Pink Buses to Offer Women Safe Public Transportation in KP. *Pakistan Forward*. 28 August.
[153] R. Khan. 2012. Pink Bus Service: Three Women-only Buses Launched. *The Express Tribune*. 5 January.
[154] In 2023, the "Pink Bus Service" also started in Karachi. See: *Ary News*. 2023. "First-Ever" Women-Only Pink Bus Service Launched in Karachi. 1 February.

Pollution

The lack of wastewater treatment facilities and the uncontrolled dumping of domestic and industrial waste have severely polluted Pakistan's aquifers and aquatic ecosystems and have contaminated drinking water distribution networks. Air pollution is also a major issue for most cities.

Pakistan ranked last out of 180 countries in the 2022 Environmental Performance Index's air quality category, which measures air pollution's direct impacts on human health based on three indicators: inhalable particulate matter (PM2.5) exposure, solid household fuels, and ozone exposure.[155] Lahore was ranked first, while Peshawar was the fifth most polluted city globally in relation to suspended matter.[156] Lahore ranked 12th on dense smog, a particular problem in winter. Overall, a rapid increase in the number of vehicles, inefficient automotive technology, dirty fuels, uncontrolled industrial emissions, and the burning of garbage account for the deterioration of air quality in Pakistani cities (footnote 35).

Noise pollution is also reaching unsafe levels in large cities. In Karachi, a mean value of 95.75-decibel noise has been observed in commercial areas during rush hour, well above the 85-decibel limit recommended to prevent hearing loss.[157]

---

[155] M.J. Wolf et al. 2022. Environmental Performance Index. Yale Center for Environmental Law and Policy.
[156] IQAir. World's Most Polluted Cities 2017–2023.
[157] J. Khan et al. 2018. Road Traffic Air and Noise Pollution Exposure Assessment—A Review of Tools and Techniques. *The Science of The Total Environment*. 634.

Urban Development Analysis

Land Use Management

Rapid urban population growth has led to the unplanned sprawling of Pakistan's cities. The country's official urbanization rate of 2.7% in 2022 ranked third in South Asia;[158] however, this may be grossly underestimated given the rigid urban–rural classification that excludes fast-growing peri-urban areas from official statistics. Government officials interviewed during this assessment suggested that the hidden and unaccounted-for urban population could have been as high as 60% of Pakistan's official urban population in 2020. The failure to adequately plan to allocate land and public infrastructure to meet the needs of a growing urban population has given rise to a sprawling and messy urbanization where public infrastructure is forced to follow, rather than lead, its residents.

Issues Across Cities

Holistic, long-term plans are lacking. Government authorities in rapidly urbanizing areas are so focused on meeting the needs of their existing residents that they have neither time nor resources to plan strategically for their future. Land use plans are either nonexistent, not followed, or quickly become obsolete. In the absence of a responsible and capable coordinating municipal authority, the fragmentation of land use planning and management across multiple siloed organizations with ambiguous and overlapping functions fails to deliver a cohesive bundle of social and economic opportunities for urban citizens.

The livability of cities is decreasing. Urban centers in Pakistan are increasingly inefficient, scoring low on multiple competitiveness indexes (footnote 35). Urban centers are also congested, unattractive, and polluted. Most urban centers lack a designated downtown area to host and encourage economic, social, and cultural activities. The few green spaces in urban centers are disappearing, while any greening projects tend to be concentrated in affluent areas. Public space has been continuously shrinking, with the increased sale of public property prompted by the high commercial value of urban land and the growing financial needs of urban authorities (footnote 37), aided by the politician–developer nexus (footnote 121).

Zoning laws limit mixed-use development. Development zoning is a common feature of the planning of Pakistani cities, but mixed-use development plans are rare. According to the Pakistan Institute for Development Economics, the country's zoning laws require immediate transformation. The institute notes that: "There are two zoning categories (in Pakistan): residential, which allows only single-family housing; and commercial, which covers everything else. Commercialization is also on a plot-by-plot basis at a large financial cost called a commercialization fee. Building regulations are stringent, discouraging high-rise, dense, and mixed-use development, resulting in limited supply and visibly excess demand for schooling, offices, shops,

---

[158] Nepal, at 3.8%, had the highest urbanization rate in South Asia in 2022; followed by Bangladesh at 3.0%. See: World Bank. Data. Urban Population Growth (Annual %) – Pakistan, Bangladesh, Bhutan, etc. (accessed 18 August 2023).

warehousing, etc."[159] These zoning laws have facilitated urban sprawl, ad hoc commercialization, and routine noncompliance in land development including unauthorized land use changes, construction without proper permits, and disregard of building codes and standards in practically all Pakistani cities.

Segregated housing patterns give rise to growing insecurity. As prime land within urban centers tends to be controlled by civil servants, judges, and army officials, the land available for mixed-use, high-rise development is limited. Middle and upper-income groups tend to live in gated residential communities or cantonments with better services, creating a stark contrast with the conditions of those living outside those communities and giving rise to a growing level of insecurity, as evidenced in the rise of security firms.

Urban sprawl has been uncontained. Urban sprawl has been exacerbated by insufficient safeguards around urban and property development in rural areas. Urban sprawl, particularly notable in major cities like Karachi and Lahore, has been accelerated by inadequate enforcement of land conversion regulations and the inability to impose municipal service costs on property developers. The associated pressure on the release of public land, or the approval of urban development on private rural land, has created perverse incentives for government officials and given rise to a land mafia. The rapid private urbanization of agricultural land, coupled with a reliance on personal vehicles for commuting in the absence of public transport systems, has led to increased congestion, pollution, and commuting costs.

Weak urban governance is facilitated by complexity. A combination of overlapping jurisdictions, unclear responsibilities, and complex procedures for decision-making on land development has undermined urban governance. This has increased lobbying by interest groups and the nonobservance of city bylaws. Illegal developments have taken advantage of a slow justice system to build settlements, and afterwards through political pressure managed to get them legalized. The political and military elite as well as private housing societies pushing for single-family housing and low-density developments contribute to unregulated urban expansions. With the demand for such development only rising, it is hard to foresee a decisive end to urban sprawl without a fundamental shift in urban planning and governance.

Recent Government Initiatives

The federal government, led by the Planning Commission, and the provincial housing and public health engineering departments are promoting vertical development. In major cities like Karachi, Lahore, and Faisalabad, building codes are being amended to enable the development of medium-rise and multi-story buildings. However, progress has been hindered by the absence of real incentives for people to move from single-family houses to high-rise apartment buildings.

With cities in Pakistan currently preparing new master plans or updating existing ones, there is an opportunity to direct land use and management toward more sustainable pathways. Forging a common understanding and the political will to address the drivers that control access to land is an essential first step. This first step needs careful consideration, recognizing that these drivers stem from age-old inequalities in land distribution that have enabled those with greater endowments to counter any attempt to dilute their economic, social, and political power, and grip over (state) resources (footnote 37).

While urban centers in Pakistan all face similar development challenges, there are some fundamental differences in urbanization issues between the four provinces and major cities.

---

[159] Pakistan Institute of Development Economics. 2020. *Framework for Economic Growth Pakistan*.

Megacities—Karachi and Lahore

Karachi and Lahore have each reached megacity status and continue to grow. The population of Karachi almost doubled over the past 2 decades leading to 2022, while that of Lahore rose by 138%. The demographic pressure on these two cities needs to be eased by developing alternative urban centers and improving the socioeconomic opportunities and living conditions in rural areas.

Karachi

Karachi is a major business hub and the financial powerhouse of Pakistan, attracting people from all over the country. While the latest available census data placed the city's population at 14.9 million, city officials in interviews for this assessment believe it may have reached 22 million–25 million by 2017. As the city expands, the availability of resources per capita is shrinking, with over 50% of Karachi's population estimated to live in informal settlements, even encroaching into the coastline's mangrove forests (footnote 117). Municipal infrastructure is outdated, service delivery systems are limited, and access to sufficient safe water is a serious concern.

With increased financial assistance and support from development partners and greater private sector involvement, some services had started to improve before the COVID-19 pandemic. Privatized K-Electric has reduced load shedding, installed meters, and increased revenue collections. The establishment of the Sindh Solid Waste Management Board and outsourcing has improved waste collection in parts of the city. The BRT lines will not completely solve the city's severe and ever-worsening traffic congestion problems but may offer some improvements.

Class division is a major problem in Karachi. Most of the elite live in cantonment areas or private housing societies, while those on low incomes have been pushed to the city's largest district, Karachi East. The city is further divided along religious and ethnic lines, which has led to several outbreaks of violence in the past.

The major socioeconomic issues in Karachi are rooted in long-standing political differences between the provincial and city governments. For this reason, the devolution of funds and functionaries to the city has been poor. On the contrary, the provincial government has centralized the services of about 15 authorities that control much of the public land and infrastructure of Karachi. Many city authorities, like the Karachi Metropolitan Corporation with a 12,000-strong workforce, and the Karachi Development Authority, have been stripped of responsibilities yet continue to be maintained with a limited mandate.[160]

The complicated political situation in the city and consequent constraints in decision-making have taken their toll on various issues, including preventive and adaptive measures to prepare for disasters triggered by natural hazards. In 2020, the city suffered the worst flooding in its history. While rains were more intense than usual, the severity of the flooding was primarily due to mismanagement—river channels and drains were blocked, not having been cleaned for at least 20 years. With climate change impacts only intensifying, risks of further disasters are escalating.[161]

Karachi is the only city in Pakistan that, to some degree, is expanding vertically due to limited land and urgent housing needs. Although there are no coordinated initiatives for vertical development, it is common for new residential buildings to be over 15 floors. However, in the last 5 years, the construction industry's attention has

---

[160] For political reasons, according to interviews conducted by this assessment's consultants.
[161] For example, on 27 August 2020, the single-day rainfall in Karachi was 223.5 millimeters, against its average annual rainfall of 170 millimeters. Summers are also becoming longer and hotter. Since 1960, Karachi's nighttime temperature has increased by approximately 2.4°C, while daytime temperatures are up by 1.6°C. See: N.H. Anwar et al. 2022. *Designed To Fail? Heat Governance In Urban South Asia: The Case Of Karachi A Scoping Study*. Edinburgh Research Archive.

shifted to the city's exurbs. Several massive new urban developments create a linear city along the Karachi–Hyderabad highway. Some of these developments are run by public or military agencies, like the Defence Housing Authority City Karachi or the Airports Security Force City. These new developments could offer relief from Karachi's pressing overpopulation and infrastructure issues. However, planned mostly as single-family housing, and car-dependent neighborhoods, they cater mainly to the upper middle-class, providing them an opportunity to escape the megacity.

Lahore

Lahore, the second-largest metropolitan after Karachi, is also the country's fastest-growing major city. The 2017 census put the population at 11.1 million, but city officials estimated that the number may have reached 13 million to 15 million.

Uncontrollable sprawl is the main challenge facing Lahore. The city is quickly absorbing surrounding agricultural fields through numerous uncoordinated housing schemes and with little central planning. Many developments are illegal and there is no mechanism to report and stop early construction. The city missed an opportunity to set its newly constructed Ring Road as a boundary and transform the road into an economic corridor, adding value to the local economy. Lahore is expanding horizontally, and this situation will not change if developers can continue to buy inexpensive agricultural land and convert it to residential plots at will. Awareness of the value of agricultural land and the potential impact of encroachment on food security should be fostered at the institutional and societal levels.

Pollution is a major issue for Lahore. Smog is common, and untreated sewage contaminates surface water and groundwater resources. Once well known for its gardens, the city has lost 10%–15% of its green areas in the last 20 years. Under the federal government's tree planting initiative, a small urban forest was created in Liberty Park at the heart of the city's commercial center, a model the urban authorities plan to replicate in more locations. The city is handicapped in addressing its environmental problems as environmental monitoring and enforcement falls under the jurisdiction of the Environmental Protection Department at the provincial level. The city is also vulnerable to flooding due to its flat topography, but as the Ravi River water level has receded, there have been no severe floods since 1988.

When it comes to municipal services, Lahore is doing better in some sectors than other cities in the country. The introduction of a mass transit system was an important improvement in urban mobility. Water supply and waste management have improved. Waste collection has significantly improved over the last few years, with operations outsourced to foreign operators and later to local private sector contractors. This has helped the capacity development of the local waste management industry. Sewerage remains an issue, but wastewater treatment plants are in the city's development plan.

Steps have been made toward protecting the rich heritage of Lahore, known as the cultural capital of Pakistan. With the support of development partners, the Walled City of Lahore Development Authority has completed restoration works within the Walled City, but several historic buildings are still under threat.

Urban planning in Lahore started earlier than in most other Pakistani cities. Following the recommendation of Pakistan's Second Five-Year Plan, preparation by a master plan committee of the Greater Lahore Master Plan began in 1961. Completed in 1966, it was not approved until 1972, by which time data had become obsolete and unauthorized development had occurred. Key shortcomings included reliance on outdated maps from 1939–1940, a drafting committee dominated by bureaucrats with insufficient town planners, secondary data for projections, lack of public involvement, and an inadequate number of planners for implementation. By 1998, a new Integrated Master Plan 2021 was proposed. However, adoption of the plan was significantly delayed due to the overlapping jurisdictions between the Lahore Development Authority and the city district government that necessitated revisions. Eventually adopted in October 2004, implementation of the plan is further challenged by the involvement of the Punjab Housing and Town Planning Agency, which adds another layer of complexity and creates ambiguity in the municipal planning process.

Over the years, Lahore's planning landscape continued to be dynamic, with the Lahore Development Authority's jurisdiction redefined in 2021 to focus solely on the metropolitan area. The adjustment occurred amid the development of a broader Master Plan for Lahore Division 2050, which covers Lahore, Sheikhupura, Kasur, and Nankana Sahib and considers various urban development projects. Overlaps in the responsibilities of the Lahore Development Authority and local governments in this master plan 2050, already approved by the Cabinet, need to be resolved to facilitate effective implementation. Local governments and other stakeholders also need to be consulted on how the plans should be implemented.

Other Major Cities

Peshawar

Peshawar experienced big waves of migration from Afghanistan during the Cold War and the 2001 global war on terror, reshaping the city's urban fabric and socioeconomic dynamics. During the first wave, informal settlements emerged without sanitation facilities. Many people stopped abiding by the law, poverty and illiteracy rates increased, and the city faced enormous social challenges.

While provincial governments then focused on improving safety and law and order, in more recent years, attention shifted to rehabilitating municipal infrastructure and planning with the support of international partners. However, demographic pressure has intensified with the merger of KP and the federally administered tribal areas, precipitating significant migration from these areas to the city. As a result, Peshawar's population doubled between 1998 and 2017.

Data from the 2021 nighttime lights study carried out by the Government of KP and development partners (footnote 18) confirmed the continuing expansion of the city. The expansion, mostly unplanned, has occurred informally as an accumulation of rural settlements with linear growth across major intercity roads. The only government-planned expansions are the model towns in Hayatabad and Regi developed by the Peshawar Development Authority as typical suburban single-family housing schemes. The KP Urban Policy 2030, adopted in early 2023, now guides the development of Peshawar (footnote 74). The city's infrastructure is improving, and the operationalization of the first BRT line in 2020 has eased traffic and boosted urban mobility.

Quetta

Although cities in Balochistan are less developed, the provincial capital, Quetta, is in relatively better condition. The city has two main urban authorities: the Quetta Development Authority, in charge of the development of residential schemes and commercial centers; and the Metropolitan Corporation Quetta, looking after municipal services. The Quetta Cantonment Board oversees local government services in the cantonment area. In addition, over 20 private housing schemes are operating in the city.

Quetta faces severe water scarcity, and its main infrastructure and service networks, including for sewage disposal, energy supply, and public transport, have limited reach and service functionalities. A master plan prepared in 1985 was barely implemented. Efforts to update the 1985 master plan were rolled out in 2020 but at the time of writing in 2023 has not yet been completed.

Resembling an agglomeration of rural settlements, Quetta's residential neighborhoods are dominated by traditional single-floor courtyard houses. The downtown areas are overpopulated and congested. Surrounded by mountains, the city has only limited space to expand, mainly to the northwest and south. An earthquake in 1935 caused mass destruction, and since then allowable building height is only up to 9.14 meters. The city's building codes are currently being revised to better respond to the increasing lack of space and the federal government's call for more vertical development.

While Quetta is directly threatened by climate change, it receives limited support from international organizations and there is no collaboration with other provinces for knowledge transfer. Private investment also remains limited and no PPP projects are planned. One bright spot is that public safety, a long-time concern, has improved in recent years.

Islamabad

Islamabad was developed following the distinctive gridiron pattern master plan formulated in the 1960s by the renowned Greek architect and urban planner, Constantinos Apostolou Doxiadis. It is considered the greenest and best-served large city in the country, with the CDA as developer and regulator. The city consists of five parts with clear zoning between them. Zone 1 is a residential and mixed-use area, with the CDA in charge of land acquisition and infrastructure development. Zone 3, the Margalla Hills National Park, is restricted for wildlife conservation, while the private sector is allowed to participate in housing development in Zones 2 and 5. As envisaged in the master plan, Zone 4 is the site of a national park, major educational institutions, and agro-industrial and research and development activities.

Until 2015, the CDA was also responsible for municipal services in the city. Under the capital territory's Local Government Act (LGA) of 2015, these functions were delegated to a new entity, the Metropolitan Corporation Islamabad. However, due to mismanagement caused by a lack of capacity and experience, the responsibility of municipal services was returned to the CDA in 2020.

The 1960s master plan is currently under review, with the gridiron pattern being considered for application in additional sectors or grids other than in Zone 1 and Zone 2. Overall, the gridiron pattern is considered successful. Although designed as a low-rise, low-density city, Islamabad is under constant pressure to deviate from the plan due to mounting housing demand. In 2023, the CDA amended the 2020 Building Control Regulations to increase permissible building heights and density in several sectors.

Like Pakistan's other major cities, the main problem in Islamabad is institutional. Instead of cooperating under a central metropolitan authority, agencies act as rivals and struggle for power. Moreover, although Islamabad and neighboring Rawalpindi City are interdependent, they have different administrative bodies, planning systems, and policies, with each following its master plan.

Good Practices

Pakistan's urban development will benefit from best practices serving as prototypes for replication across the country. From planning and implementation to maintenance after completion, there are good examples the sector can build upon to improve service delivery and enhance development effectiveness and impact. It will also be important for Pakistan's development practitioners to consider informing and guiding urban policy and strategy, investment planning, project implementation, and institutional strengthening with approaches that have proved viable and are applicable to their needs and contexts.

Decentralization

KP decentralization process. By amending the province's LGA of 2019 and abolishing the district council, the KP government has put in place an institutional framework for improved efficiency and greater autonomy to the cities. The flatter, two-tier governance system will also bring city institutions within easier reach of their constituencies.

Private Sector Participation

Chamber of Commerce, Sialkot. In Punjab, the contribution of the Chamber of Commerce of Sialkot to the city's infrastructure development is exemplary. Through a PPP agreement, the chamber and the city government worked together to develop the city's road and water supply networks on a 50–50 funding partnership basis. Although the government stopped its funding after 10% progress, the chamber continued financing the project. The chamber has also funded a dry port and the city's airport and recently launched a private airline.

Modern Infrastructure

Mass transit projects. Mass transit projects are important additions to the transport infrastructure of Pakistani cities. The Green Line BRT of Lahore and the BRT of Peshawar are among the most successful BRT schemes when it comes to ridership and route alignment.

The Orange Line in Lahore, the first metro line in the country, can significantly improve urban mobility and living conditions. The initial controversy regarding its high capital cost and criticisms about its final alignment and station locations need to be carefully examined in efforts to replicate the model. The proposed but ultimately dropped mixed-use commercial and residential high-density zones had the potential to transform Lahore through transit-oriented development.

Heritage Conservation and Protection

Lahore Walled City restoration. The Walled City of Lahore Authority carried out its restoration project in cooperation with several development partners and the Aga Khan Trust for Culture. It is one of the few ongoing heritage projects of its scale in Pakistan that preserves historic culture, enhances resilience, and boosts the local economy.

ADB in Pakistan

Since 1966, ADB has supported 22 urban and water sector projects in Pakistan worth $2.137 billion.[162] ADB's early sector assistance focused on improving urban infrastructure and services, particularly in water supply, sanitation, and solid waste management. In recent years, it has taken more integrated approaches, combining reforms and investments to help build livable cities that are green, inclusive, resilient, and competitive.[163] Tightening synergy and coordination with ADB-supported initiatives in other sectors; strengthening capacities in planning, including addressing climate change and disaster risks; and greater emphasis on gender equality, knowledge solutions, and innovation have bolstered ADB's shift toward integrated urban development solutions.[164]

---

[162] ADB. 2024. Pakistan. Asian Development Member Fact Sheet. April.
[163] ADB. 2020. Country Partnership Strategy: Pakistan, 2021–2025—Lifting Growth, Building Resilience, Increasing Competitiveness.
[164] This shift has become most prominent with the adoption by ADB of Strategy 2030 in 2018.

The 12 completed lending projects have shown mixed performances. Project completion reports point to common key factors behind shortfalls and failures, including poor ownership of projects by the government and other key stakeholders and limited capacity in the implementing agencies. Inadequate procurement and contract management capacities and land acquisition issues have also slowed project implementation, often resulting in low loan utilization and cancellation. Experiences of both successful and unsuccessful projects provide good lessons for the urban sector in Pakistan (Box 1).

To address the low loan utilization encountered in several past projects, ADB has supported the operationalization of a new instrument, the project readiness financing facility.[165] This instrument, assisting the provinces in investment planning, feasibility study, and detailed design since 2019, has proved effective in facilitating project preparation, enhancing readiness, and minimizing implementation delays.

> ### Box 1: Lessons from Project Success and Failure in the Urban Sector of Pakistan
>
> **Case 1: The Punjab Community Water Supply and Sanitation Project**
>
> This 2003–2006 implemented project stands out as the only urban loan in Pakistan rated *highly successful* in its project completion report (PCR).
>
> The PCR attributes the project's successful implementation, "primarily (to) its design, which accounted for on-the-ground realities, applied lessons from previous interventions, and incorporated and adopted efficient and sustainable delivery mechanisms. Involvement (of) beneficiaries in the project process(es)… was key to the success of the subprojects. Training, awareness raising, and capacity building of beneficiaries (were) also instrumental in ensuring the sustainability of (sub)projects… owned and operated by the communities. Appointing qualified staff and retaining them for the project's duration avoided delays in implementation. The active support of the provincial government and of senior EA (executing agency) management helped smooth implementation."
>
> **Case 2: The Sindh Cities Improvement Investment Program**
>
> This program, a multitranche financing facility approved for up to $300 million in December 2008, was originally designed to provide five tranches of individual loans to support the establishment and professionalization of a state-owned urban utility company in the province. However, due to delays and lack of commitment from the provincial government, the program ended up disbursing only two loans. The 2019 PCR rated the program *unsuccessful*, citing the indecisiveness of the government on the direction of the utility company as the principal reason for the termination of the facility.
>
> The PCR highlights the following key lesson: "Although the 2001 devolution reforms provided scope for more effective service provision, continued overlap and fragmentation of responsibilities between the local government and provincial agencies constrained improvements. Alternative approaches are required to (enhance urban) service provision, including separating service delivery needs from political interests, professionalizing urban management, and outsourcing to private sector and introducing cost-recovery tariff regimes to ensure sustainable operations."
>
> Sources: ADB. 2008. *Project Completion Report: Punjab Community Water Supply and Sanitation Sector Project* and ADB. 2019. *Project Completion Report: MFF Sindh Cities Improvement Investment Program*.

---

[165] Including Pakistan: Khyber Pakhtunkhwa Cities Improvement Project–Project Readiness Financing, Pakistan: Punjab Urban Development Projects, and Pakistan: Khyber Pakhtunkhwa Cities Improvement Projects–Second Project Readiness Financing.

Urban Development Futures

Pakistan is at a critical juncture. Urban aggregation, arguably the key driver of economic and social development in Pakistan, is challenged by failing public services, declining quality of life, and flagging economic productivity. The impetus underwriting the current urban development model of maximizing economic growth, while seeking to mitigate the associated social and environmental impacts, is encountering immense challenges due to low compliance and weak regulation.

This national urban assessment has identified the need for a sustainable urban development model that seeks to internalize the economic, environmental, and social benefits associated with higher levels of agglomeration. The new model will need to be characterized by robust planning and evaluation capacities that extend vertically (clearly demarcating governance responsibilities) and horizontally (internalizing multisector service requirements) as well as spatially (continuously optimizing land use) and temporally (investing financially in development needs). The unmanaged and unplanned urban sprawl currently taking place needs to be reined in by proactive institutions that underwrite the social and economic well-being of urban citizens with the public infrastructure and services necessary to sustain growth without detrimental environmental consequences. This calls for clear lines of responsibility and accountability in urban governance and well-articulated urban plans and mandates for infrastructure and service delivery that extend beyond urban areas to the urbanizing ones.

Urban Governance

A vertical urban governance model needs to advance the delineation of responsibilities vertically among the various levels of government, a process initiated by the 18th Amendment and solidified through the passage of the provincial local government acts (LGAs). While the LGAs retain the functional responsibility of urban policymaking with the provinces and transfer urban service provision to local governments, this has not been accompanied by the strengthening of institutional capacity among local governments to manage these services. To date, the provinces have made little progress in relinquishing control over the funds or the functionaries that deliver urban services. The provinces have also failed to streamline the many overlapping agencies with unclear mandates and competing interests, which has led to inefficient governance and weak citizen engagement. The resulting inadequacies in urban planning and municipal service delivery have been most acute in the peri-urban areas hosting a fast-growing urban population hidden by the nebulous urban–rural classification in official statistical systems.

Separating the regulation of failure (by provincial governments) from the licensing of compliance (by local governments), the delivery of urban services (by publicly or privately owned providers), and the arbitration of disputes (by local government commissions), as well as creating well-defined obligations and reporting lines, can facilitate the vertically and horizontally delineated urban governance model alluded to in various provincial LGAs.

- **The regulation of failure** requires a provincial government to focus on establishing laws and regulations, policies, and standards for all the subsectors related to urban development (e.g., transport, water supply, sewerage and drainage systems, flood management, social services, public space and recreation, housing, tourism, and commerce and industry) across the province. Departments within the provincial government can fulfill their regulatory obligations by undertaking random spot checks to identify service failures within their jurisdiction and hold local government and service providers accountable. They should also take the lead in institutional reforms to strengthen urban governance, particularly setting in place and ensuring the execution of well-delineated vertical and horizontal responsibility and accountability systems. This includes the block transfer of the quantum of funds to local governments necessary for them to perform their designated functions, along with robust regulation of their failures to do so.
- **The licensing of compliance** requires local governments to fulfill their service delivery obligations through the exercise of powers within their jurisdiction to license out or contract urban service providers (whether public or private and whether locally, provincially, or federally owned) to comply with provincial laws and regulations. Through the passage of local bylaws, urban local governments can exercise power over the implementation of land use plans, the approval or rejection of land development proposals, and the licensing of municipal service provision within their jurisdiction. Considering the rapid growth of peri-urban areas outside defined urban boundaries, neighboring local governments will need to exercise their powers to pass bylaws and contract or license urban service providers to ensure the quality of municipal services in these jurisdictions.
- **The delivery of urban services** requires downwardly accountable providers to generate revenues from their clients, invest in service improvements within the boundaries established by the local governments under contract (if local government owns the assets) or license (if local government does not own the assets), and return dividends to their owners (provincial, local government, or private). This will require continued reform of government-owned urban service providers (i.e., water and sanitation agencies, development authorities, and waste management companies), where subsidies to cover operating losses are gradually replaced by loans for viable investments or targeted transfers, subject to meeting the performance levels stipulated in the contract or license agreement. Sustained revenue generation and service improvements, actively taken up by the service providers, will reduce the burden on government to raise revenues to meet the costs of providing public services for all, enabling public finance to be prioritized for delivering services to the underserved groups (i.e., gap financing for pro-poor service delivery or as the provider of last resort).
- **The arbitration of disputes** in the interpretation of the assignment of functions, funds, and jurisdictions to local governments as prescribed in the LGA requires suitably empowered and independent arbitration entities established for this purpose within the LGAs. This includes the adjudication on the execution of the assignment of functions and functionaries by local government commissions, the execution of the horizontal and vertical assignment of funds to local governments by local government finance commissions, and the execution of electoral boundaries and processes by provincial election commissions. While the independence of legislated commissions is a lofty ambition, establishing these commissions with an appropriate balance between the brokers of local and provincial powers may be sufficient to provide the local government system with the checks and balances necessary to deliver sustainable urbanization in Pakistan.

Implementing the existing local government legislation, including adherence to legally prescribed government tenure (i.e., timely elections), will strengthen government's ability to address the vagaries of uncontrolled urbanization. In addition to strengthening the provinces' regulatory role, there is also a need to limit the subsidies to government-owned utilities, as this tends to undermine their efficiency, accountability, and financial sustainability. The licensing (permitting) or contracting (engaging) of urban service providers by local governments will empower urban local governments to exercise responsibility for the execution of master plans and the enforcement of bylaws to ensure the quality of urban services delivered by federally, provincially, and privately owned companies, authorities, and agencies. Increasing the revenues from clients of public and private urban service delivery at the municipal level will in turn strengthen the accountability of municipal local governments to their citizens.

Where possible, sustainable urban planning should seek to channel revenues from the increasing financial and economic value of the urbanization of land to the delivery of essential public services. Coupled with efforts to distribute service costs to the beneficiaries through user fees (e.g., road tolls and metered water), the increasing public revenues from the urban development of land should lead to the continued enhancement and expansion of services and a consequent spiral in revenue sources. By linking service liabilities with the financial investments made by speculative urban service providers and by mandating social and environmental provisions in property developments, the ongoing budget pressures on local governments can gradually ease. This easing of budget pressure should enable municipalities to shift toward the strategic budgeting of plans that deliver higher social, economic, and environmental benefits and which can potentially free up resources for the provision of vital social safety nets.

The importance of multisector technical competency in supporting the urbanization agenda has been recognized with the establishment of urban units in three of the four provinces. It is important to assign the urban units a mandated role and empower them with technical competency to provide knowledge and advisory services that respond to the needs of both provincial and local governments. This implies an institutional arrangement where urban units are mandated by provincial governments while also accountable to elected local governments, and an administration that is sufficiently independent to engage high-caliber professionals from the market.

A national urban unit comprising a coalition of provincial governments could be established to support the urbanization agenda. This could be achieved through a corporate entity with majority representation by provincial urban departments and minority representation from the Ministry of Climate Change and Environmental Coordination (MOCC&EC). Services offered to provinces should include but not be limited to drafting urban policies and implementation guidelines, building knowledge, strengthening urban development capacities, stocktaking and sharing local and international best practices, unifying standards, and benchmarking progress. A majority provincially owned national urban unit can assist the MOCC&EC to target and report on the country's international obligations that relate to urbanization managed by the provinces. Budgets for the provision of technical urban services to the provinces and federal government could be sourced from a mixture of annual contributions stipulated in the shareholding agreement and fees for services to respective provincial and federal governments. A corporate structure and fee for service charges should enable the engagement of professionals on competitive market-based contracts as demonstrated by the Urban Unit in Punjab. This may also offer a model that could be replicated to garner learning and support for the devolution processes undertaken by the provincial governments in the wake of the 18th Amendment.

Sustainable Urban Planning

The piecemeal and reactive approach to urban development needs to shift to a forward-looking approach that offers integrated solutions to the challenges arising from urbanization. The emphasis on planning alluded to in this assessment is not a renewed focus on urban planning, but a multisector planning approach that fosters the allocation of land, capital, and labor across conventional boundaries to maximize the social, environmental, and economic returns for all.

Existing LGAs in the different provinces already empower local governments to pass urban bylaws, approve land use plans, and exercise control over development proposals. The continual and progressive redefinition of land use approval requirements in peri-urban areas (including transport corridors and industry hubs) is essential to enable public infrastructure to guide and respond to urbanization trends, rather than continually chase messy urbanization repairing socially, environmentally, and technically inadequate urban services.

Regular assessments of urbanization trends (i.e., increases in housing and transport densities, decreases in green spaces, and evolution of business areas) will be necessary to inform the reclassification of land use approval requirements as development imperatives and opportunities evolve. The staging of development planning (i.e., process of dividing large-scale development projects into smaller, more manageable stages) would also need to outline the division of responsibilities (whether municipality or developer) in the provision of public, environmental, and social services in accordance with local bylaws, zoning regulations, and the nature of the prospective development.

Overlaying revisions to land use plans in urban and peri-urban areas with detailed multisector infrastructure master plans and extensive consultation should enable the public and private sectors to deliver and sustain the economic, social, and environmental dividends of urbanization. These master plans should seek to minimize the environmental, social, and economic costs associated with accessing transport, housing, business, industry, education, water, and power. The importance of coordination in the development of multisector urban master plans with routine reviews of compliance and updates cannot be overstated. While public investment plans need to be coordinated by the provincial planning and development departments, the implementation of these plans needs to be managed by the local governments.

An overarching land use and master planning framework must prioritize increased population density, mixed-use developments, and pedestrian-friendly cityscapes. This should foster the creation of public and community spaces while also accommodating a broad range of urban activities that are commercial, cultural, and educational. It should also incentivize investments in high-rise, inner-city regeneration projects or the vertical redevelopment of informal settlements that can be reinforced with policies for property developers to invest in affordable housing, energy efficiency, and green spaces.

Because of the country's vulnerability to climate change, Pakistan needs to prioritize climate-resilient interventions in urban areas. The streetscape and public spaces in Pakistani cities need to be reinvented, increasing walkability, green spaces, and recreational areas. Natural drainage channels must be cleared of encroachments and regularly cleaned to facilitate groundwater recharge. Vertical and horizontal greening needs to be high on the agenda to reduce the urban heat island effect. Climate-resilient urban development will require climate risk and vulnerability assessments in the planning and project development stage. The Climate Change Act and the National Climate Change Policy provide the mandate for both federal and provincial agencies to institutionalize climate screening of all development projects, regardless of funding sources.

Socially inclusive and environmentally sustainable urbanization calls for progressive reforms in the following areas:

- **Real estate tax reform.** Currently, capital gains on open plots remain tax-exempt after a 6-year holding period, while constructed properties incur zero tax after 4 years. While incentivizing outward property development into peri-urban areas and depriving the government of much-needed revenues, these tax exemption policies encourage speculative investments in real estate directing investments away from productive sectors (e.g., manufacturing and agri-business) and inhibiting the country's potential for higher growth and productivity. Thwarting the unmanaged urban expansion necessitates standard taxation on immovable property sales and investments.

- **Energy reform.** While energy is a federal responsibility, provincial and local governments have a critical role to play in demand-side management to improve energy efficiency and conservation. Urban master plans and bylaws need to prioritize energy efficiency in water supply, transport systems, and building design, promote the use of renewable energy sources and energy-efficient heating and cooling, and lay the groundwork for modern communication technologies in commercial areas, homes, and offices.
- **Water supply reform.** Improving access to safe drinking water across all cities requires a long-term integrated water resources management plan to preserve watersheds and aquifers, promote water saving and reuse, and reduce nonrevenue water. Wastewater treatment and proper disposal need to be put in operation with strict monitoring and penalties applied to deter environmentally harmful practices.
- **Solid waste reform.** Improving solid waste management requires the establishment of a legal and regulatory framework for the collection and proper disposal of various types of waste (e.g., municipal, electronic, industrial, and hospital); the provision of adequate collection and disposal services, including environmentally sound facilities at disposal sites; and intensive education campaigns to facilitate a shift in societal thinking and behavior toward more efficient resource use, following the circular economy model's reduce, reuse, and recycle (3R) approach. Incentivizing waste-to-energy, polluters pay, and zero-waste initiatives could accelerate the reform process.
- **Transport reform.** Transport and urban development are intertwined and mutually reinforcing. Strong alignment between urban land use planning and transport development is essential. Urban planning should prioritize the establishment of vibrant, mixed-use communities around public transportation hubs, while transport development should prioritize the creation of sustainable and livable urban spaces where people can live, work, and access amenities with minimal reliance on private vehicles. Planning that minimizes transit distances and maximizes connectivity will necessitate the deployment of multiple transport modalities.

Role of Development Partners

Development partners have an important role to play in urban development, particularly through knowledge sharing and development financing. Strengthening coordination among development partners will bring concerted efforts to realize the benefits of urbanization and the required institutional reforms to carry forward the urban agenda. Coordination processes with development partners led by governments at the federal, provincial, and local levels will increase knowledge sharing, reduce overlap, and maintain consistency.

Under *Strategy 2030*, ADB has shifted its focus to integrated approaches for urban development. ADB envisions a proactive role in advocating and supporting sustainable urban development models. Urban governance reforms stand as a key focus area. ADB aims to integrate climate considerations into planning, improve revenue generation, and reform budget frameworks. It also acknowledges the significance of project readiness and context-specific reforms for successful implementation.

ADB's historical successes in public sector management highlight the importance of focused initiatives, though further engagement in local governance and decentralization initiatives is warranted. This approach has sought to enhance the coverage, quality, efficiency, and reliability of municipal services; strengthen urban planning and financial sustainability of cities; and improve the urban environment, enhance climate resilience, and bolster disaster risk management capacity. By increasing collaboration, local engagement, and strategic governance reforms, this approach aims to improve sustainable and resilient urban development into the future.

Urban Development Scenarios

Pakistan has significant comparative advantages it can build on to create a more prosperous economy and better future for its people. The country has a young and dynamic population and a rising urban, educated, and skilled middle class. It has strong research institutions and is strategically located to become a regional hub for trade and economic activity. Freeing cities from their binding logistic, social, and environmental constraints to growth is an essential prerequisite to harness these comparative advantages for development. Targeted scenarios and the required actions to manage the transition to a new development model are outlined below. The identified actions are further fleshed out in Box 2.

Short-Term Scenario (1 to 10 years)

- Strengthen municipal authority to approve and enforce risk-informed development plans and license urban services
- Strengthen local government capacity for increasing own-source revenue, gender-responsive budgeting and expenditure, and strengthening operation and maintenance systems
- Update existing urban master plans as risk-informed urban master plans requiring routine compliance or revisions
- Institutionalize a culture of accountability in local, provincial, and federal governments
- Pilot PPP agreements defining municipal service delivery standards
- Strengthen provincial departmental capacity to identify service delivery failures
- Enhance financial sustainability through cost-recovery mechanisms among service providers
- Launch an urban regeneration project centered on high-density and mixed-use development

Medium-Term Scenario (10 to 20 years)

- Scale up PPP agreements for the delivery of different municipal services
- Expand the high-density regeneration model across cities with private sector involvement
- Scale up e-governance and smart city applications
- Enhance the independence and capacity of local government commissions

Long-Term Scenario (20 to 30 years)

- Create competitive, resilient, and sustainable urban centers
- Foster economic, social, and cultural activities in regenerated urban centers
- Embed circular economy principles in urban planning and development
- Leverage demographic dividends and empower women in economically competitive urban centers

Box 2: Summary of Proposed Action Points

Vertical and Horizontal Urban Governance

- Implement pieces of provincial legislation that decentralize the responsibility for municipal service delivery to local government.
- Enhance this decentralization process by providing fiscal independence and increasing the revenue assignment to urban local governments.
- Support urban local governments in revenue generation, including robust billing and collection mechanisms and sharing of revenues from ring-fenced municipal utilities.
- Strengthen arbitration commissions to maintain fairness and transparency in local government elections, fiscal transfers, and staffing levels.
- Reform institutional relationships to reduce the overlaps in urban governance. This demands the clear delineation of roles and responsibilities between provincial departments and local governments.
- Support all local governments to strengthen consistency of and compliance with urban bylaws, including adopting more stringent environmental and social clauses and greater restrictions on urban sprawl.
- Increase the level of awareness regarding climate change and its impacts and sensitize policy makers and institutions.
- Forge climate change alliances and partnerships with countries and/or organizations in the region.
- Update policies, programs, and implementation frameworks relevant to national climate change response and integrate them into urban service delivery and planning processes.
- Adopt and scale up the application of digital technologies in urban governance and service delivery.

Vertical and Horizontal Urban Planning

- Formulate and execute city master plans with frequent reviews and amendments in response to new developments.
- Provide incentives to urban local governments to implement their master plans, including fiscal transfers for implementation and penalties for failure.
- Develop a common and shared database of assets and services between all public agencies at the city level (i.e., development authorities, municipal corporations, water and sanitation agencies).
- Conduct national censuses at a regular interval of no more than 10 years. Prepare comprehensive population projections combined with an analysis of depleting natural resources to support planning.
- Develop a federal policy document on urban planning to harmonize and create consistency between federal and provincial regulations.
- Propose a polycentric growth approach to balance urban development between the provinces and reduce pressure on megacities. Examine the need for planning new cities or satellite towns.
- Advance climate-resilient water, sanitation, and hygiene initiatives using nature-based solutions, regulations, cross-sector collaboration, and habitat preservation that contribute to a lower carbon footprint.
- Develop and adopt an equitable housing policy to tackle densification, quality of life, and affordability issues. This should include the housing needs of marginalized populations and scaling of successful *katchi abadi*[a] upgrading models along with *katchi abadi* regularization programs.
- Provide incentives and a new regulatory framework for private sector participation in the delivery of municipal services, affordable housing, and operation and maintenance of existing infrastructure.
- Provide the legislative framework and incentives for vertical development in urban centers, reforming the mortgage regime and incentivizing the private sector to include affordable housing.
- Promote the adoption of an ecosystem approach to recover and develop the former fragile urban sector into a stronger and more resilient sector.
- Give greater attention to infrastructure development and service delivery in small and medium-sized cities to reduce monocentric development and ease pressure on megacities.
- Disincentivize investments in development that encroach upon agricultural lands and embed targeted policy measure in the regulatory framework and taxation system.

[a] *Katchi abadis* are informal settlements formed by homeless people, mostly from low-income groups, to establish temporary abodes typically under substandard living conditions.

Source: Asian Development Bank project team and consultants.

Appendix

Pakistan's Budget Allocation Systems

Public Expenditure and Financial Accountability (PEFA) reports, initiated by international donors, provide a snapshot of a country's performance in public financial management (PFM). They are based on a framework and methodology now recognized as the global standard for PFM assessment and have been used in the Asian Development Bank (ADB) national urban assessment in Pakistan as the main reference and basis for all information and analyses related to the budget allocation systems. ADB has been a contributor to all the PEFA reports that, in the case of Pakistan, have varying timelines at the province level.[1]

Federal Level

The Planning Commission (PC) is the highest federal body of Pakistan responsible for preparing the national economic and social development plans and the federal government's annual Public Sector Development Programme (PSDP). In addition, it coordinates with the provincial governments the approval of development projects and issues guidelines for public investment management.

The guidelines for reviewing capital investment projects are laid out in the *Planning Commission: Manual for Development Projects* that all the provinces have adopted. The manual sets the responsibilities for planning, approving, implementing, and evaluating development and/or investment projects. It further defines the planning documents and responsible departments and describes the steps to be followed at the federal and provincial levels in planning, implementing, and evaluating projects.

The manual prescribes the following set of templates or PC proformas to be used at each stage of the project cycle:

- PC Proforma I (PC-I): for project appraisal and economic analysis. A simplified version of PC-I is required for small, nonrecurring projects valued at up to PRs1 million.
- PC-II: for detailed feasibility studies to justify large projects. PC-II, prepared before PC-I, is also used for soft interventions, such as capacity-building programs and surveys.
- PC-III: for quarterly monitoring and reporting of ongoing projects to be accomplished by either the executing, sponsoring, or implementation agencies. PC-III is expected to cover physical and financial progress and report implementation issues.
- PC-IV: for handover of projects from the executing, sponsoring, or implementing agencies to the requesting, parent, or user departments.
- PC-V: for end-of-project and/or program evaluation, to be prepared annually for 5 years.

---

[1] Province-level information used in this Appendix is available at https://www.pefa.org/country/pakistan and dated as follows: Balochistan = 2017, Khyber Pakhtunkhwa =2017, Sindh = 2013, Punjab =2012.

The guidelines for reviewing capital investment projects (development budget) are included in the PC manual. At appraisal stage, the guidelines require new projects to include the following four sections:

- Project information, name, implementing entity, completion period, a summary of costs details, and project objectives.
- Project description and justification, location, market analysis, technical description, operating or recurrent cost estimates, capital cost estimates, unit costs, sectoral benefits, cash flow, financing arrangements, foreign exchange component, risk analysis, and participation of beneficiaries.
- Project requirements such as human resources, physical and other facilities, materials, supplies, and equipment.
- Environmental aspects, including impact assessment e.g., on water, sewage, and solid waste and recommendations to mitigate environmental pollution.

Province Level

In all four provinces, the Planning and Development (P&D) Department is the leading and coordinating unit for planning. It allocates funds, sets priorities, and oversees the various development sectors. It facilitates and guides the government cabinets in decision-making. Each department submits its annual development plan (ADP) to the P&D for review and approval, prior to the provincial assembly's final approval. However, depending on funding size, the approval of projects may be done in lower tiers.

Sindh. The preparation, implementation, and monitoring of the development budget in Sindh province is an independent exercise that has little synchronization with sector strategies and the availability of development funds. This has created the risk of suboptimal use of resources for development purposes.

The Finance Department has a dominant role in budget preparation and compiles the budget following defined timetables and after discussions with the line departments. The P&D Department is responsible for preparing and monitoring the ADP. The budget is brought to the provincial legislature for review and approval. Drawing and disbursing officers, nominated in spending departments, submit expenditure bills to the accounts offices for payment. The district- and provincial-level accounts offices process payment claims while exercising budgetary controls and compliance checks. According to the legal framework, the controller general of accounts, through the provincial accountant general, maintains the financial transaction accounts and prepares financial reports—both in-year and the annual financial statements of Sindh province. The auditor general of Pakistan externally audits the accounts, and the audited accounts and related management letters are submitted to the provincial governor. The latter then brings these before the provincial legislature for scrutiny.

The Sindh Provincial Finance Commission constituted in 2001, is empowered to devise a formula for distributing resources among the districts. The formula covers both development transfers and current transfers. Recent transfers have sought to maintain the supply of existing services to minimize intra-district poverty and inter-district income differential by maintaining the supply of existing services and development grants in the districts at an equitable level.

The district governments formed under the Sindh Local Government Ordinance (SLGO) 2001 had political representation. The SLGO also empowered the district governments to prepare their budget and manage their education, health care, and other subjects under their purview. The 2001 SLGO was repealed in 2011 and the 1979 commissioner system of district governments was revived. This has resulted in an eventually non-devolved district government structure.

Budgeting for investment carried out by the P&D Department and budgeting for recurrent costs at the Finance Department are parallel. It would benefit greatly from a higher level of integration.

Without the appropriate forum approving the development scheme, no expenditure can be committed to the development side. The rules further require feasibility reports for any project over PRs300 million as a prerequisite for inclusion in the ADP. Moreover, no development scheme can be approved unless proper and timely financing is available. These controls, although comprehensive, are often not strictly adhered to, or exceptional procedures are invoked. Documentary evidence of the fulfillment of all these requirements is not always available. Since the departments have no reliable information for committing expenditures, the commitments are much more than the available funds in most cases. Once the ADP is approved, the P&D Department does not have discretion regarding prioritization.

A public–private partnership (PPP) cell has been established within the Economic Reform Unit with the support of ADB. The Sindh Public–Private Partnership Act 2010 mandates the PPP Policy Board to develop PPP policies and projects in the province. The cell acts as secretariat to the board and provides technical assistance and advice to the concerned agencies and line departments throughout the project preparation cycle. Several development projects involving the private sector have been undertaken in the province.

Punjab. Based on the 2012 PEFA report, budget preparation in Punjab has historically been primarily short-run, input-focused, and incremental with little prioritization of expenditures. The use of the budget as a tool for implementing strategies toward achieving the government's policy goals has been limited. Still, in the last few years, the Government of Punjab has been implementing a multiyear budget process, the Medium-Term Budgetary Framework (MTBF), including some performance targets to implement the longer-term development strategies envisioned in its *2020 Vision and the Punjab Growth Strategy 2023*.

The MTBF is a multiyear budgeting approach that links the government's budget plans to its policy objectives over the medium term, usually 3 years. By introducing a medium–term horizon to the budgeting process, the process becomes more strategic and responsive to the government's priorities. The principal objectives of the MTBF are to

- link the availability of estimated resources with the Medium–Term Fiscal Framework and fiscal policy initiatives;
- strengthen financial discipline in the management/execution of the budget;
- align budgetary allocations and expenditures with the policies and priorities of the government; and
- ensure efficiency and cost-effectiveness in the use of public sector resources.

The PFM process at the provincial level starts with budget preparation. After discussing with the line departments, the Finance Department compiles the budget according to defined timetables. This budget is then presented to the provincial legislature for review and approval. Drawing and disbursing officers in the spending departments submit expenditure bills to the accounts offices for payment. The accounts offices at the district and provincial levels process payment claims and exercise budgetary controls and compliance checks. In accordance with the legal framework and through the provincial attorney-general, the Controller General of Accounts maintains the financial accounts and prepares the financial reports—both in-year and the annual financial statements for the Province of Punjab. The Accountant General of Punjab audits the accounts, submits the audited accounts and related management letters to the Punjab governor, then brings these to the provincial legislature for scrutiny.

The allocations from the provincial to local governments are determined through a consultative process steered by the Provincial Finance Commission, a body with 10 members representing the Punjab district governments and private sector. The commission uses a formula, called the Provincial Finance Commission Award, to ensure equitable and transparent allocations based on various economic and social indicators, e.g., population and development level. The amount to be allocated to local governments is 41.9% of the net proceeds of the provincial consolidated fund in every financial year. A further division within each tier is based on formulas linked to grant types, population, and relevant indices. Grant types include general purpose grants, equalization grants, development grants, and tied grants. The breakdown is that city and/or district governments receive 83.81%, *tehsils* (subdistricts) and/or town municipal administrations get 12.50%, and union administrations receive 3.69%. More than 80% of the district budget comprises salaries.

The estimates for foreign-assisted budgets are forecast by the project-executing agencies based on the donors' program and schedule of aid agreed upon with the donors. The foreign aid section of the P&D Department then consolidates the input for inclusion in the ADP. The executing agencies prepare the project feasibility documentation (PC-II) for approval by the P&D Department and other agencies as required. The planned expenditures are included in the development budget of the province.

The *Punjab Growth Strategy 2023* recognizes the need for a gender-sensitive budget. The strategy states, "Improving the human capital development, unless it incorporates almost half of the population, would not be possible. For Punjab to move toward the true model of human capital development, women's development and its related interventions need to be identified and brought up at the time when projects, especially in health, education, employment, and skills, are being planned and financed. Women empowerment and women development programs that would eventually become part of the Annual Development Programmes of the province – should include gender-based observations."[2]

Khyber Pakhtunkhwa (KP). The P&D Department, headed by the additional chief secretary, is the principal planning organization at the KP provincial level. It steers the provincial public investment program (development budget) and coordinates, screens, and reviews the development proposals prepared by the line departments. Project identification and selection take place at the sponsoring agencies and are reviewed by the P&D Department at the Provincial Development Working Party (PDWP), the highest provincial forum mandated to appraise and approve project proposals. Projects can be developed and financed from the province's ADP, but only up to a particular ceiling. Projects up to PRs5 billion are also reviewed and approved by the federal government. Pre-PDWP meetings are held among the line departments and the P&D sections to review the technical details of project proposals.

The *Planning Commission: Manual for Development Projects* stipulates that appraisal of development projects depends on the government's economic policies, then on the rate of return (financial and economic), in addition to considerations of social and environmental impacts and risks. Due to their complexity and size, the government involves donors for financial and technical assistance in most major investment projects; therefore, all such projects must comply with a strict appraisal process. However, no clear guidance exists on whether there are considerations of alternative projects before selecting the ones that get funded.

---

[2] Government of Punjab. Planning and Development Board. (Undated). *Punjab Growth Strategy 2023*, p. 119.

Moreover, though very few, there were instances in the last few years where large projects were included in the provincial portfolio after the approval of the annual budget by the provincial assembly (legislature). Commonly referred to as non-ADP schemes, such projects were submitted for legislative approval in the revised budget estimates. Economic analysis of the major investment decisions within the provincial remit is conducted independently by the P&D Department through the PDWP. However, the detailed project analysis and its results are not published.

The provincial portfolio includes large and complex projects. Small projects, numbering in the hundreds, evade formal project document preparation and appraisal. The practice of inclusion of "unapproved schemes" (project proposals not screened by the PDWP) is common. As a result, project prioritization and appraisal are undermined. Many development projects included in the ADP are small projects that neither qualify as a capital investment (some are training, some relate to operation and maintenance [O&M] costs) nor are large enough to warrant a due process and feasibility review. Sponsoring agencies for such projects as well as many of those in the budget do not systematically comply with the due process requirement for economic, financial, social, and sustainability analysis to be undertaken as part of PC-I and PC-II documentation.

The provincial ADP includes umbrella schemes that cannot comprehensively screen proposals for targeted interventions. A close look at these umbrella schemes in terms of targeted beneficiaries and geographic locations would reveal how they add to the already enormous number of projects in the provincial portfolio, making planning, review, monitoring, and evaluation challenging.

Most of the significant investment projects of the Government of KP follow the appraisal and prioritization process. The scrutiny is higher for donor-funded projects, since the proposals are reviewed by the provincial and federal governments and must comply with the donor review requirements, which entail a detailed multidimensional appraisal and selection process. A feasibility study and detailed project costing are parts of PC-I or PC-II, depending on the nature of each project.

The Government of KP, like other provincial governments, has designated the P&D Department as responsible for the development (investment) budget and the Financial Department for the current (recurrent) budget. It prepares medium-term fiscal and budgetary frameworks that provide estimates for the budget year and subsequent 2 years. The estimated cost is broken down per cost category for the project duration; however, the project planning documents focus on the capital (development) budget and do not integrate the recurrent costs or analyze the impact of the project after completion on the recurrent budget. Lack of compliance with the federal-level PC guidelines in estimating the costs of ongoing and new projects and allocative inefficiencies result in the funding needed to complete projects being brought forward for disbursement at later dates.

Under the current decentralized scheme, 30% of the provincial government's budget goes to local governments. Adding grants to utility companies brings this amount to more than 40%. With that budget, local governments have improved their level of delivery of municipal services such as water supply, sanitation, and building control.

Balochistan. The province has a centralized public investment management system. As with the other provinces of Pakistan, its P&D Department, led by the additional chief secretary, is the provincial principal planning organization. The department directs the provincial public investments covered by the federal development budget and the PSDP and coordinates, screens, and reviews the project proposals prepared by the sponsoring agencies and line departments. Project identification and selection take place at line departments and are reviewed by the P&D Department at the PDWP, the highest provincial forum mandated to appraise and approve the project proposals. Projects up to a ceiling of PRs5 billion can be developed, appraised, and financed from the province's ADP. Foreign-funded projects and projects over PRs5 billion are reviewed and approved by the federal government.

The PC manual requires the preparation of PC-I for the appraisal of development projects. However, sponsoring agencies and line departments do not carry out the needed due process before including projects in the budget. The Balochistan Budget Manual 1987 only allows the inclusion of an unapproved scheme in the development budget on an exceptional basis and with the approval of the secretaries of finance and planning.

Many development projects included in the PSDP are small and do not qualify as capital investment but are also not large enough to warrant a due process and feasibility review. The average size of a development project is about $300,000.

The development budget is approved on a lump-sum basis without due appraisal and costing of the projects. An unwritten and informal policy of the Government of Balochistan is that each of the 65 members of the provincial assembly can include new projects or schemes in the PSDP for up to PRs300 million per year. These projects are only identified less than two months before presenting the budget to the legislature when there is not enough time for project appraisal or feasibility.

After approval of the budget, PC-I documents including economic analysis are prepared and approved by the provincial government. As part of the appraisal, the review of economic analysis is not thorough due to the limited capacity of the P&D Department. Moreover, the appraisal becomes insignificant as projects have already been approved along with the budget. However, sponsoring agencies are not allowed to incur expenditure on development projects until the approval of PC-I. The projects' appraisal and PC-I documents are not published.

According to the PC manual, the P&D Department coordinates the development programs prepared by the provincial departments and prepares the overall provincial 5-year annual plans. Despite the clear guidance issued by the PC concerning the selection of development projects, there are no publicly available medium- and long-term development plans for the province to be used as the basis for the investment budget and project approval process. In addition, there is no clear guidance on whether there should be considerations of alternative projects before making the final selection of projects that get funded. There is also no evidence that a given project idea or concept undergoes any sort of preliminary assessment to decide whether developing it further into a detailed project proposal would be worth the effort.

The sponsoring agencies primarily make the selection of projects. Further reviews by the P&D Department only focus on the funding available for the year and are not based on preestablished selection criteria for arbitrage among the competing projects.

The PC guidelines require that project appraisal include the estimates of both the investments and annual O&M costs for the duration of the projects. However, in practice, PC-I documents mainly include capital cost estimates with little or no information about O&M costs. Moreover, as PC-I documents are prepared and approved after the approval of the budget by the legislature, the capital costs may not be fully estimated. Development and recurrent budgets are prepared separately, and there is no multiyear budget framework.

As in other provinces, notification of completion is made through a document known as the Statement of New Expenditure issued by the project sponsoring agency and submitted to the Finance Department. Only then can O&M costs be included in the annual budget. Their financing, however, is subject to the availability of funding as determined by the department. Total capital cost, projection of total capital cost, and current-year budget allocation for each project are provided in the published PSDP budget documents. However, the projected capital cost is for the project's entire life, and the capital cost for the forthcoming budget year is not available in the budget documents.

On the revenue side, fiscal transfers from the federal government constitute more than 90% of provincial receipts, guaranteed under the 7th National Finance Commission Award. The National Finance Commission award is a revenue-sharing arrangement that allows the provinces to receive budgetary allocations from a pool of tax and nontax collections that go directly to the federal government. Own-source revenue targets are prepared without a long-term view and careful analysis.

The Government of Balochistan has been unable to achieve revenue collection targets for the last few fiscal years. There is limited public disclosure of budgetary information and serious concerns about the integrity of financial data. It also has not formulated a system for transparent and rules-based fiscal transfers to the local governments. Deficient public debt management, public assets management, and fiscal risk reporting contribute to weak aggregate fiscal discipline.

No mechanism or practice exists to monitor financial performance and risk arising from public corporations and local governments; a complete list of government-owned public corporations is unavailable. Contingent liabilities are neither monitored nor reported. There is no consolidated reporting of fixed assets, nor is there any proper mechanism for appraising the performance of fixed assets. This ultimately contributes to the poor maintenance of capital assets that shorten their useful life.

The only budget monitoring within the Government of Balochistan is done with minimal scope by the P&D Department's monitoring wing. However, the monitoring is not adequately carried out due to limited staff and other resources. In the absence of internal audits or any other monitoring of fiscal issues, effective monitoring of the Finance Department's utilization of public money is difficult.

The Government of Balochistan has no approved strategic development plan to prioritize resource allocation and measure development impact. Moreover, there is no practice of adopting and communicating budget ceilings to sectors/departments. Under the current situation, development projects are given a budget without proper costing, appraisal, or approval. There are no established criteria for project selection and guidelines for project identification and assessment are not followed. Information systems within the line departments are either weak or nonexistent and result in duplication of public investments in one area and no investments in other places where they are needed. Employee-related expenses consume about 75% of the budget, limiting the availability of expenditure.

www.ingramcontent.com/pod-product-compliance
Lightning Source LLC
Chambersburg PA
CBHW040930240426
43667CB00027B/3001